# THE
# Essentials
# OF
# Prayer

# THE
# Essentials
## OF
# Prayer

## E. M. BOUNDS

**MOODY PRESS**

**CHICAGO**

MOODY PRESS EDITION, 1980
ISBN 0-8024-6723-7

# Contents

# I

## PRAYER TAKES IN THE WHOLE MAN

"Henry Clay Trumbull spoke forth the Infinite in the terms of our world, and the Eternal in the forms of our human life. Some years ago, on a ferry-boat, I met a gentleman who knew him, and I told him that when I had last seen Dr. Trumbull, a fortnight before, he had spoken of him. 'Oh, yes,' said my friend, "he was a great Christian, so real, so intense. He was at my home years ago and we were talking about prayer." "Why, Trumbull," I said, "you don't mean to say if you lost a pencil you would pray about it, and ask God to help you find it." "Of course I would; of course I would," was his instant and excited reply.' Of course he would. Was not his faith a real thing? Like the Saviour, he put his doctrine strongly by taking an extreme illustration to embody his principle, but the principle was fundamental. He did trust God in everything. And the Father honoured the trust of His child."—ROBERT E. SPEER

PRAYER has to do with the entire man. Prayer takes in man in his whole being, mind, soul and body. It takes the whole man to pray, and prayer affects the entire man in its gracious results. As the whole nature of man enters into prayer, so also all that belongs to man is the beneficiary of prayer. All of man receives benefits in prayer. The whole man must be given to God in praying. The largest results in praying come to him who gives himself, all of himself, all that belongs to himself, to God. This is the secret of full consecration, and this is a condition of successful praying, and the sort of praying which brings the largest fruits.

The men of olden times who wrought well in prayer, who brought the largest things to pass, who moved God to do great things, were those who were entirely given over to God in their praying. God wants, and must have, all that there is in man in answering his prayers. He must have wholehearted men through whom to work out His purposes and plans concerning men. God must have men in their entirety. No double-minded man need apply. No vacillating man can be used. No man with a divided allegiance to God, and the world and self, can do the praying that is needed.

Holiness is wholeness, and so God wants holy men, men whole-hearted and true, for His service and for the work of praying. "And the very God of peace sanctify you wholly; and I pray God your whole spirit and soul and body be preserved blameless unto the coming of our Lord Jesus Christ." These are the sort of men God wants for leaders of the hosts of Israel, and these are the kind out of which the praying class is formed.

Man is a trinity in one, and yet man is neither a trinity nor a dual creature when he prays, but a unit. Man is one in all the essentials and acts and attitudes of piety. Soul, spirit and body are to unite in all things pertaining to life and godliness.

The body, first of all, engages in prayer, since it assumes the praying attitude in prayer. Prostration of the body becomes us in praying as well as prostration of the soul. The attitude of the body counts much in prayer, although it is true that the heart may be haughty and lifted up, and the mind listless and wandering, and the praying a mere form, even while the knees are bent in prayer.

Daniel kneeled upon his knees three times a day in prayer. Solomon kneeled in prayer at the dedication of the temple. Our Lord in Gethsemane prostrated Himself in that memorable season of praying just before His betrayal. Where there is earnest and faithful praying the body always takes on the form most suited to the state of the soul at the time. The body, that far, joins the soul in praying.

The entire man must pray. The whole man, life, heart, temper, mind, are in it. Each and all join in the prayer exercise. Doubt, double-mindedness, division of the affections, are all foreign to the closet. Character and conduct, undefiled, made whiter than snow, are mighty potencies, and are the most seemly beauties for the closet hour, and for the struggles of prayer.

A loyal intellect must conspire and add the energy and fire of its undoubting and undivided faith to that kind of an hour, the hour of prayer. Necessarily the mind enters into the praying. First of all, it takes thought to pray. The intellect teaches us we ought to pray. By serious thinking beforehand the mind prepares itself for approaching a throne of grace. Thought goes before entrance into the closet and prepares the way for true praying. It considers what will be asked for in the closet hour. True praying does not leave to the inspiration of the hour what will be the requests of that hour. As praying is asking for something definite of God, so, beforehand, the thought arises —" What shall I ask for at this hour? " All vain and evil and frivolous thoughts are eliminated, and the mind is given over entirely to God, thinking of Him, of what is needed, and what has been received in the past. By every token, prayer, in taking hold of the entire man, does not leave out the mind. The very first step in prayer is a mental one. The disciples took that first step when they said unto Jesus at one time, " Lord, teach us to pray." We must be taught through the intellect, and just in so far as the intellect is given up to God in prayer, will we be able to learn well and readily the lesson of prayer.

Paul spreads the nature of prayer over the whole man. It must be so. It takes the whole man to embrace in its god-like sympathies the entire race of man—the sorrows, the sins and the death of Adam's fallen race. It takes the whole man to run parallel with God's high and sublime will in saving mankind. It takes the whole man to stand with our Lord Jesus Christ as the one Mediator between God and sinful man. This is the doctrine Paul teaches in his prayer-directory in the second chapter of his first Epistle to Timothy.

Nowhere does it appear so clearly that it requires the entire man in all departments of his being, to pray than in this teaching of Paul. It takes the whole man to pray till all the storms which agitate his soul are calmed to a great calm, till the stormy winds and waves cease as by a Godlike spell. It takes the whole man to pray till cruel tyrants and unjust rulers are changed in their natures and lives, as well as in their governing qualities, or till they cease to rule. It requires the entire man in praying till high and proud and unspiritual ecclesiastics become gentle, lowly and religious, till godliness and gravity bear rule in Church and in State, in home and in business, in public as well as in private life.

It is man's business to pray; and it takes manly men to do it. It is godly business to pray and it takes godly men to do it. And it is godly men who give over themselves entirely to prayer. Prayer is far-reaching in its influence and in its gracious effects. It is intense and profound business which deals with God and His plans and purposes, and it takes whole-hearted men to do it. No half-hearted, half-brained, half-spirited effort will do for this serious, all-important, heavenly business. The whole heart, the whole brain, the whole spirit, must be in the matter of praying, which is so mightily to affect the characters and destinies of men.

The answer of Jesus to the scribe as to what was the first and greatest commandment was as follows:

" The Lord our God is one Lord; And thou shalt love the Lord thy God with all thy heart, and with thy soul, and with all thy mind, and with all thy strength."

In one word, the entire man without reservation must love God. So it takes the same entire man to do the praying which God requires of men. All the powers of man must be engaged in it. God cannot tolerate a divided heart in the love He requires of men, neither can He bear with a divided man in praying.

In the one hundred and nineteenth Psalm the Psalmist teaches this very truth in these words:

" Blessed are they that keep his testimonies, and that seek him with the whole heart."

It takes whole-hearted men to keep God's commandments and it demands the same sort of men to seek God. These are they who are counted " blessed." Upon these whole-hearted ones God's approval rests.

Bringing the case closer home to himself the Psalmist makes this declaration as to his practice: " With my whole heart have I sought thee; O let me not wander from thy commandments."

And further on, giving us his prayer for a wise

and understanding heart, he tells us his purposes concerning the keeping of God's law:

" Give me understanding and I shall keep thy law; Yea, I shall observe it with my whole heart."

Just as it requires a whole heart given to God to gladly and fully obey God's commandments, so it takes a whole heart to do effectual praying.

Because it requires the whole man to pray, praying is no easy task. Praying is far more than simply bending the knee and saying a few words by rote.

> " 'Tis not enough to bend the knee,
>     And words of prayer to say;
>   The heart must with the lips agree,
>     Or else we do not pray."

Praying is no light and trifling exercise. While children should be taught early to pray, praying is no child's task. Prayer draws upon the whole nature of man. Prayer engages all the powers of man's moral and spiritual nature. It is this which explains somewhat the praying of our Lord described as in Hebrews 5:7:

" Who in the days of his flesh, when he had offered up prayers and supplications, with strong crying and tears, unto him that was able to save him from death, and was heard in that he feared."

It takes only a moment's thought to see how such

praying of our Lord drew mightily upon all the powers of His being, and called into exercise every part of His nature. This is the praying which brings the soul close to God and which brings God down to earth.

Body, soul and spirit are taxed and brought under tribute to prayer. David Brainerd makes this record of his praying:

" God enabled me to agonise in prayer till I was wet with perspiration, though in the shade and in a cool place."

The Son of God in Gethsemane was in an agony of prayer, which engaged His whole being:

" And when he was at the place, he said unto them, Pray ye that ye enter not into temptation. And he was withdrawn from them about a stone's cast, and kneeled down and prayed, saying, Father, if thou be willing, remove this cup from me; nevertheless, not my will, but thine, be done. And there appeared an angel unto him, from heaven, strengthening him. And being in an agony, he prayed more earnestly: and his sweat was as it were great drops of blood falling down to the ground." Luke 22 : 40-44.

Here was praying which laid its hands on every part of our Lord's nature, which called forth all the powers of his soul, His mind and His body. This was praying which took in the entire man.

Paul was acquainted with this kind of praying. In writing to the Roman Christians, he urges them to pray with him after this fashion:

"Now I beseech you, brethren, for the Lord Jesus Christ's sake, and for the love of the Spirit, that ye strive together with me in your prayers to God for me."

The words, "strive together with me," tells of Paul's praying, and how much he put into it. It is not a docile request, not a little thing, this sort of praying, this "striving with me." It is of the nature of a great battle, a conflict to win, a great battle to be fought. The praying Christian, as the soldier, fights a life-and-death struggle. His honour, his immortality, and eternal life are all in it. This is praying as the athlete struggles for the mastery, and for the crown, and as he wrestles or runs a race. Everything depends on the strength he puts in it. Energy, ardour, swiftness, every power of his nature is in it. Every power is quickened and strained to its very utmost. Littleness, half-heartedness, weakness and laziness are all absent.

Just as it takes the whole man to pray successfully, so in turn the whole man receives the benefits of such praying. As every part of man's complex being enters into true praying, so every part of that same nature receives blessings from God in answer to such praying. This kind of praying engages our undivided hearts, our full consent to be the Lord's, our whole desires.

God sees to it that when the whole man prays, in turn the whole man shall be blessed. His body takes in the good of praying, for much praying is done specifically for the body. Food and raiment, health and bodily vigour, come in answer to praying. Clear mental action, right thinking, an enlightened understanding, and safe reasoning powers, come from praying. Divine guidance means God so moving and impressing the mind, that we shall make wise and safe decisions. "The meek will he guide in judgment."

Many a praying preacher has been greatly helped just at this point. The unction of the Holy One which comes upon the preacher invigorates the mind, loosens up thought and gives utterance. This is the explanation of former days when men of very limited education had such wonderful liberty of the Spirit in praying and in preaching. Their thoughts flowed as a stream of water. Their entire intellectual machinery felt the impulse of the Divine Spirit's gracious influences.

And, of course, the soul receives large benefits in this sort of praying. Thousands can testify to this statement. So we repeat, that as the entire man comes into play in true, earnest effectual praying, so the entire man, soul, mind and body, receives the benefits of prayer.

# II

# PRAYER AND HUMILITY

"If two angels were to receive at the same moment a commission from God, one to go down and rule earth's grandest empire, the other to go and sweep the streets of its meanest village, it would be a matter of entire indifference to each which service fell to his lot, the post of ruler or the post of scavenger; for the joy of the angels lies only in obedience to God's will, and with equal joy they would lift a Lazarus in his rags to Abraham's bosom, or be a chariot of fire to carry an Elijah home."—JOHN NEWTON

TO be humble is to have a low estimate of one's self. It is to be modest, lowly, with a disposition to seek obscurity. Humility retires itself from the public gaze. It does not seek publicity nor hunt for high places, neither does it care for prominence. Humility is retiring in its nature. Self-abasement belongs to humility. It is given to self-depreciation. It never exalts itself in the eyes of others nor even in the eyes of itself. Modesty is one of its most prominent characteristics.

In humility there is the total absence of pride, and it is at the very farthest distance from anything like self-conceit. There is no self-praise in humility. Rather it has the disposition to praise others. "In honour preferring one another." It is not given to self-exaltation. Humility does not love the uppermost seats and aspire to the high places. It is willing to take the lowliest seat and prefers those places where it will be unnoticed. The prayer of humility is after this fashion:

> " Never let the world break in,
> Fix a mighty gulf between ;
> Keep me humble and unknown,
> Prized and loved by God alone."

Humility does not have its eyes on self, but rather on God and others. It is poor in spirit, meek in behaviour, lowly in heart. " With all lowliness and meekness, with long-suffering, forbearing one another in love."

The parable of the Pharisee and publican is a sermon in brief on humility and self-praise. The Pharisee, given over to self-conceit, wrapped up in himself, seeing only his own self-righteous deeds, catalogues his virtues before God, despising the poor publican who stands afar off. He exalts himself, gives himself over to self-praise, is self-centered, and goes away unjustified, condemned and rejected by God.

The publican sees no good in himself, is overwhelmed with self-depreciation, far removed from anything which would take any credit for any good in himself, does not presume to lift his eyes to heaven, but with downcast countenance smites himself on his breast, and cries out, " God be merciful to me, a sinner."

Our Lord with great preciseness gives us the sequel of the story of these two men, one utterly devoid of humility, the other utterly submerged in the spirit of self-depreciation and lowliness of mind.

" I tell you this man went down to his house justified rather than the other; for every one that exalteth himself shall be abased; and he that humbleth himself shall be exalted." Luke 18:14.

God puts a great price on humility of heart. It is good to be clothed with humility as with a garment. It is written, " God resisteth the proud, but giveth grace to the humble." That which brings the praying soul near to God is humility of heart. That which gives wings to prayer is lowliness of mind. That which gives ready access to the throne of grace is self-depreciation. Pride, self-esteem, and self-praise effectually shut the door of prayer. He who would come to God must approach Him with self hid from his eyes. He must not be puffed-up with self-conceit, nor be possessed with an over-estimate of his virtues and good works.

Humility is a rare Christian grace, of great price in the courts of heaven, entering into and being an inseparable condition of effectual praying. It gives access to God when other qualities fail. It takes many descriptions to describe it, and many definitions to define it. It is a rare and retiring grace. Its full portrait is found only in the Lord Jesus

Christ. Our prayers must be set low before they can ever rise high. Our prayers must have much of the dust on them before they can ever have much of the glory of the skies in them. In our Lord's teaching, humility has such prominence in His system of religion, and is such a distinguishing feature of His character, that to leave it out of His lesson on prayer would be very unseemly, would not comport with His character, and would not fit into His religious system.

The parable of the Pharisee and publican stands out in such bold relief that we must again refer to it. The Pharisee seemed to be inured to prayer. Certainly he should have known by that time how to pray, but alas! like many others, he seemed never to have learned this invaluable lesson. He leaves business and business hours and walks with steady and fixed steps up to the house of prayer. The position and place are well-chosen by him. There is the sacred place, the sacred hour, and the sacred name, each and all invoked by this seemingly praying man. But this praying ecclesiastic, though schooled to prayer, by training and by habit, prays not. Words are uttered by him, but words are not prayer. God hears his words only to condemn him. A death-chill has come from those formal lips of prayer—a death-curse from God is on his words of prayer. A solution of pride has entirely poisoned the prayer offering of that hour. His entire praying has been impregnated with self-praise, self-congratulation, and self-exaltation. That season of temple going has had no worship whatever in it.

On the other hand, the publican, smitten with a deep sense of his sins and his inward sinfulness, realising how poor in spirit he is, how utterly devoid of anything like righteousness, goodness, or any quality which would commend him to God, his pride within utterly blasted and dead, falls down with humiliation and despair before God, while he utters a sharp cry for mercy for his sins and his guilt. A sense of sin and a realisation of utter unworthiness has fixed the roots of humility deep down in his soul, and has oppressed self and eye and heart, downward to the dust. This is the picture of humility against pride in praying. Here we see by sharp contrast the utter worthlessness of self-righteousness, self-exaltation, and self-praise in praying, and the great value, the beauty and the Divine commendation which comes to humility of heart, self-depreciation, and self-condemnation when a soul comes before God in prayer.

Happy are they who have no righteousness of their own to plead and no goodness of their own of which to boast. Humility flourishes in the soil of a true and deep sense of our sinfulness and our nothingness. Nowhere does humility grow so rankly and so rapidly and shine so brilliantly, as when it feels all guilty, confesses all sin, and trusts all grace. " I the chief of sinners am, but Jesus died for me." That is praying ground, the ground of humility, low down, far away seemingly, but in reality brought nigh by the blood of the Lord Jesus Christ. God dwells in the lowly places. He makes such lowly places really the high places to the praying soul.

> " Let the world their virtue boast,
>     Their works of righteousness;
> I, a wretch undone and lost,
>     Am freely saved by grace;
> Other title I disclaim,
>     This, only this, is all my plea,
> I the chief of sinners am,
>     But Jesus died for me."

Humility is an indispensable requisite of true prayer. It must be an attribute, a characteristic of prayer. Humility must be in the praying character as light is in the sun. Prayer has no beginning, no ending, no being, without humility. As a ship is made for the sea, so prayer is made for humility, and so humility is made for prayer.

Humility is not abstraction from self, nor does it ignore thought about self. It is a many-phased principle. Humility is born by looking at God, and His holiness, and then looking at self and man's unholiness. Humility loves obscurity and silence, dreads applause, esteems the virtues of others, excuses their faults with mildness, easily pardons injuries, fears contempt less and less, and sees baseness and falsehood in pride. A true nobleness and greatness are in humility. It knows and reveres the inestimable riches of the Cross, and the humiliations of Jesus Christ. It fears the lustre of those virtues admired by men, and loves those that are more secret and which are prized by God. It draws comfort even from its own defects, through the abasement which they occasion. It prefers any degree of compunction before all light in the world.

Somewhat after this order of description is that definable grace of humility, so perfectly drawn in the publican's prayer, and so entirely absent from the prayer of the Pharisee. It takes many sittings to make a good picture of it.

Humility holds in its keeping the very life of prayer. Neither pride nor vanity can pray. Humility, though, is much more than the absence of vanity and pride. It is a positive quality, a substantial force, which energises prayer. There is no power in prayer to ascend without it. Humility springs from a lowly estimate of ourselves and of our deservings. The Pharisee prayed not, though well schooled and habituated to pray, because there was no humility in his praying. The publican prayed, though banned by the public and receiving no encouragement from Church sentiment, because he prayed in humility. To be clothed with humility is to be clothed with a praying garment. Humility is just feeling little because we *are* little. Humility is realising our unworthiness because we *are* unworthy, the feeling and declaring ourselves sinners because we *are* sinners. Kneeling well becomes us as the attitude of prayer, because it betokens humility.

The Pharisee's proud estimate of himself and his supreme contempt for his neighbour closed the gates of prayer to him, while humility opened wide those gates to the defamed and reviled publican.

That fearful saying of our Lord about the works of big, religious workers in the latter part of the Sermon on the Mount, is called out by proud estimates of work and wrong estimates of prayer:

" Many shall say unto me in that day, Lord, Lord, have we not prophesied in thy name? and in thy name cast out devils? and in thy name done many wonderful works? And then will I profess unto them, I never knew you: depart from me, ye that work iniquity."

Humility is the first and last attribute of Christly religion, and the first and last attribute of Christly praying. There is no Christ without humility. There is no praying without humility. If thou wouldst learn well the art of praying, then learn well the lesson of humility.

How graceful and imperative does the attitude of humility become to us! Humility is one of the unchanging and exacting attitudes of prayer. Dust, ashes, earth upon the head, sackcloth for the body, and fasting for the appetites, were the sym-

bols of humility for the Old Testament saints.
Sackcloth, fasting and ashes brought Daniel a low-
liness before God, and brought Gabriel to him.
The angels are fond of the sackcloth-and-ashes men.

How lowly the attitude of Abraham, the friend
of God, when pleading for God to stay His wrath
against Sodom! "Which am but sackcloth and
ashes." With what humility does Solomon appear
before God! His grandeur is abased, and his glory
and majesty are retired as he assumes the rightful
attitude before God: "I am but a little child, and
know not how to go out or to come in."

The pride of doing sends its poison all through
our praying. The same pride of being infects all
our prayers, no matter how well-worded they may
be. It was this lack of humility, this self-applaud-
ing, this self-exaltation, which kept the most religious man of Christ's day from being accepted of
God. And the same thing will keep us in this day
from being accepted of Him.

> "O that now I might decrease!
> O that all I am might cease!
> Let me into nothing fall!
> Let my Lord be all in all."

# III

## PRAYER AND DEVOTION

"Once as I rode out into the woods for my health, in 1737, having alighted from my horse in a retired place, as my manner commonly had been to walk for divine contemplation and prayer, I had a view that for me was extraordinary, of the glory of the Son of God. As near as I can judge, this continued about an hour; and kept me the greater part of the time in a flood of tears and weeping aloud. I felt an ardency of soul to be what I know not otherwise how to express, emptied and annihilated; to love Him with a holy and pure love; to serve and follow Him; to be perfectly sanctified and made pure with a divine and heavenly purity."—JONATHAN EDWARDS

DEVOTION has a religious signification. The root of devotion is to devote to a sacred use. So that devotion in its true sense has to do with religious worship. It stands intimately connected with true prayer. Devotion is the particular frame of mind found in one entirely devoted to God. It is the spirit of reverence, of awe, of godly fear. It is a state of heart which appears before God in prayer and worship. It is foreign to everything like lightness of spirit, and is opposed to levity and noise and bluster. Devotion dwells in the realm of quietness and is still before God. It is serious, thoughtful, meditative.

Devotion belongs to the inner life and lives in

28

the closet, but also appears in the public services of the sanctuary. It is a part of the very spirit of true worship, and is of the nature of the spirit of prayer.

Devotion belongs to the devout man, whose thoughts and feelings are devoted to God. Such a man has a mind given up wholly to religion, and possesses a strong affection for God and an ardent love for His house. Cornelius was " a devout man, one that feared God with all his house, which gave much alms to the people, and prayed always." " Devout men carried Stephen to his burial." " One Ananias, a devout man, according to the law," was sent unto Saul when he was blind, to tell him what the Lord would have him do. God can wonderfully use such men, for devout men are His chosen agents in carrying forward His plans.

Prayer promotes the spirit of devotion, while devotion is favourable to the best praying. Devotion furthers prayer and helps to drive prayer home to the object which it seeks. Prayer thrives in the atmosphere of true devotion. It is easy to pray when in the spirit of devotion. The attitude of mind and the state of heart implied in devotion make prayer effectual in reaching the throne of grace. God dwells where the spirit of devotion resides. All the graces of the Spirit are nourished and grow well in the environment created by devotion. Indeed, these graces grow nowhere else but here. The absence of a devotional spirit means death to the graces born in a renewed heart. True worship finds congeniality in the atmosphere made by a spirit of devotion. While prayer is helpful to devotion, at the same time devotion reacts on prayer, and helps us to pray.

Devotion engages the heart in prayer. It is not an easy task for the lips to try to pray while the heart is absent from it. The charge which God at one time made against His ancient Israel was, that they honoured Him with their lips while their hearts were far from Him.

The very essence of prayer is the spirit of devotion. Without devotion prayer is an empty form, a vain round of words. Sad to say, much of this kind of prayer prevails, today, in the Church. This is a busy age, bustling and active, and this bustling spirit has invaded the Church of God. Its religious performances are many. The Church works at religion with the order, precision and force of real machinery. But too often it works with the heartlessness of the machine. There is much of the treadmill movement in our ceaseless round and routine of religious doings. We pray without praying. We sing without singing with the Spirit and the understanding. We have music without the praise of God being in it, or near it. We go to Church by habit, and come home all too gladly when the benediction is pronounced. We read our accustomed chapter in the Bible, and feel quite relieved when the task is done. We say our prayers by rote, as a schoolboy recites his lesson, and are not sorry when the Amen is uttered.

Religion has to do with everything but our hearts. It engages our hands and feet, it takes hold of our voices, it lays its hands on our money, it affects even the postures of our bodies, but it does not take hold of our affections, our desires, our zeal, and make us serious, desperately in earnest, and cause us to be quiet and worshipful in the presence of God. Social affinities attract us to the house of God, not the spirit of the occasion. Church membership keeps us after a fashion decent in outward conduct and with some shadow of loyalty to our baptismal vows, but the heart is not in the thing. It remains cold, formal, and unimpressed amid all this outward performance, while we give ourselves over to self-congratulation that we are doing wonderfully well religiously.

Why all these sad defects in our piety? Why this modern perversion of the true nature of the religion of Jesus Christ? Why is the modern type of religion so much like a jewel-case, with the precious jewels gone? Why so much of this handling religion with the hands, often not too clean or unsoiled, and so little of it felt in the heart and witnessed in the life?

The great lack of modern religion is the spirit of devotion. We hear sermons in the same spirit with which we listen to a lecture or hear a speech. We visit the house of God just as if it were a common place, on a level with the theatre, the lecture-room or the forum. We look upon the minister of God not as the divinely-called man of God, but merely as a sort of public speaker, on a plane with the politician, the lawyer, or the average speech maker, or the lecturer.  Oh, how the spirit of true and genuine devotion would radically change all this for the better!  We handle sacred things just as if they were the things of the world.  Even the sacrament of the Lord's Supper becomes a mere religious performance, no preparation for it before-hand, and no meditation and prayer afterward. Even the sacrament of Baptism has lost much of its solemnity, and degenerated into a mere form, with nothing specially in it.

We need the spirit of devotion, not only to salt our secularities, but to make praying real pray-ers.  We need to put the spirit of devotion into Monday's business as well as in Sunday's worship. We need the spirit of devotion, to recollect always the presence of God, to be always doing the will of God, to direct all things always to the glory of God.

The spirit of devotion puts God in all things.  It puts God not merely in our praying and Church going, but in all the concerns of life.  " Whether, therefore, ye eat or drink, or whatsoever ye do, do all to the glory of God."  The spirit of devotion makes the common things of earth sacred, and the little things great.  With this spirit of devotion, we go to business on Monday directed by the very same influence, and inspired by the same influences by which we went to Church on Sunday.  The spirit of devotion makes a Sabbath out of Saturday, and transforms the shop and the office into a temple of God.

The spirit of devotion removes religion from being a thin veneer, and puts it into the very life and being of our souls. With it religion ceases to be doing a mere work, and becomes a heart, sending its rich blood through every artery and beating with the pulsations of vigourous and radiant life.

The spirit of devotion is not merely the aroma of religion, but the stalk and stem on which religion grows. It is the salt which penetrates and makes savoury all religious acts. It is the sugar which sweetens duty, self-denial and sacrifice. It is the bright colouring which relieves the dullness of religious performances. It dispels frivolity and drives away all skin-deep forms of worship, and makes worship a serious and deep-seated service, impregnating body, soul and spirit with its heavenly infusion. Let us ask in all seriousness, has this highest angel of heaven, this heavenly spirit of devotion, this brightest and best angel of earth, left us? When the angel of devotion has gone, the angel of prayer has lost its wings, and it becomes a deformed and loveless thing.

The ardour of devotion is in prayer. In the fourth chapter of Revelation, verse eight, we read: " And they rest not day nor night, saying, Holy, Holy, Holy, Lord God Almighty, which was, and is, and is to come." The inspiration and centre of their rapturous devotion is the holiness of God. That holiness of God claims their attention, inflames their devotion. There is nothing cold, nothing dull, nothing wearisome about them or their heavenly worship. " They rest not day nor night." What zeal! What unfainting ardour and ceaseless rapture! The ministry of prayer, if it be anything worthy of the name, is a ministry of ardour, a ministry of unwearied and intense longing after God and after His holiness.

The spirit of devotion pervades the saints in heaven and characterizes the worship of heaven's angelic intelligences. No devotionless creatures are in that heavenly world. God is there, and His very presence begets the spirit of reverence, of awe, and of filial fear. If we would be partakers with them after death, we must first learn the spirit of devotion on earth before we get there.

These living creatures in their restless, tireless, attitude after God, and their rapt devotion to His holiness, are the perfect symbols and illustrations of true prayer and its ardour. Prayer must be aflame. Its ardour must consume. Prayer without fervour is as a sun without light or heat, or as a flower without beauty or fragrance. A soul devoted to God is a fervent soul, and prayer is the creature of that flame. He only can truly pray who is all aglow for holiness, for God, and for heaven.

Activity is not strength. Work is not zeal.

Moving about is not devotion. Activity often is the unrecognised symptom of spiritual weakness. It may be hurtful to piety when made the substitute for real devotion in worship. The colt is much more active than its mother, but she is the wheel-horse of the team, pulling the load without noise or bluster or show. The child is more active than the father, who may be bearing the rule and burdens of an empire on his heart and shoulders. Enthusiasm is more active than faith, though it cannot remove mountains nor call into action any of the omnipotent forces which faith can command.

A feeble, lively, showy religious activity may spring from many causes. There is much running around, much stirring about, much going here and there, in present-day Church life, but sad to say, the spirit of genuine, heartfelt devotion is strangely lacking. If there be real spiritual life, a deep-toned activity will spring from it. But it is an activity springing from strength and not from weakness. It is an activity which has deep roots, many and strong.

In the nature of things, religion must show much of its growth above ground. Much will be seen and be evident to the eye. The flower and fruit of a holy life, abounding in good works, must be seen. It cannot be otherwise. But the surface growth must be based on a vigourous growth of unseen life and hidden roots. Deep down in the renewed nature must the roots of religion go which is seen on the outside. The external must have a deep internal groundwork. There must be much of the invisible and the underground growth, or else the life will be feeble and short-lived, and the external growth sickly and fruitless.

In the Book of the prophet Isaiah these words are written:

"They that wait on the Lord shall renew their strength; they shall mount up with wings as eagles; they shall run and not be weary; and they shall walk and not faint." 40:31.

This is the genesis of the whole matter of activity and strength of the most energetic, exhaustless and untiring nature. All this is the result of waiting on God.

There may be much of activity induced by drill, created by enthusiasm, the product of the weakness of the flesh, the inspiration of volatile, short-lived forces. Activity is often at the expense of more solid, useful elements, and generally to the total neglect of prayer. To be too busy with God's work to commune with God, to be busy with doing Church work without taking time to talk to God about His work, is the highway to backsliding, and many people have walked therein to the hurt of their immortal souls.

Notwithstanding great activity, great enthusiasm, and much hurrah for the work, the work and the activity will be but blindness without the cultivation and the maturity of the graces of prayer.

# IV

## PRAYER, PRAISE AND THANKSGIVING

"Dr. A. J. Gordon describes the impression made upon his mind by intercourse with Joseph Rabinowitz, whom Dr. Delitzsch considered the most remarkable Jewish convert since Saul of Tarsus: 'We shall not soon forget the radiance that would come into his face as he expounded the Messianic psalms at our morning or evening worship, and how, as here and there he caught a glimpse of the suffering or glorified Christ, he would suddenly lift his hands and his eyes to heaven in a burst of adoration, exclaiming with Thomas after he had seen the nail-prints, "My Lord, and my God."'"

—D. M. McIntyre

PRAYER, praise and thanksgiving all go in company. A close relationship exists between them. Praise and thanksgiving are so near alike that it is not easy to distinguish between them or define them separately. The Scriptures join these three things together. Many are the causes for thanksgiving and praise. The Psalms are filled with many songs of praise and hymns of thanksgiving, all pointing back to the results of prayer. Thanksgiving includes gratitude. In fact thanksgiving is but the expression of an inward conscious gratitude to God for mercies received. Gratitude is an inward emotion of the soul, involuntarily arising therein, while thanksgiving is the voluntary expression of gratitude.

Thanksgiving is oral, positive, active. It is the giving out of something to God. Thanksgiving comes out into the open. Gratitude is secret, silent, negative, passive, not showing its being till expressed in praise and thanksgiving. Gratitude is felt in the heart. Thanksgiving is the expression of that inward feeling.

Thanksgiving is just what the word itself signifies—the giving of thanks to God. It is giving something to God in words which we feel at heart for blessings received. Gratitude arises from a contemplation of the goodness of God. It is bred by serious meditation on what God has done for us. Both gratitude and thanksgiving point to, and have to do with God and His mercies. The heart is consciously grateful to God. The soul gives expression to that heartfelt gratitude to God in words or acts.

Gratitude is born of meditation on God's grace and mercy. "The Lord hath done great things for us, whereof we are glad." Herein we see the value of serious meditation. "My meditation of him shall be sweet." Praise is begotten by gratitude and a conscious obligation to God for mercies given. As we think of mercies past, the heart is inwardly moved to gratitude.

> "I love to think on mercies past,
>   And future good implore;
> And all my cares and sorrows cast
>   On Him whom I adore."

Love is the child of gratitude. Love grows as gratitude is felt, and then breaks out into praise and thanksgiving to God: " I love the Lord because he hath heard my voice and my supplication." Answered prayers cause gratitude, and gratitude brings forth a love that declares it will not cease praying: " Because he hath inclined his ear unto me, therefore will I call upon him as long as I live." Gratitude and love move to larger and increased praying.

Paul appeals to the Romans to dedicate themselves wholly to God, a living sacrifice, and the constraining motive is the mercies of God:

" I beseech you, therefore, brethren, by the mercies of God, that ye present your bodies a living sacrifice, holy, acceptable unto God, which is your reasonable service."

Consideration of God's mercies not only begets gratitude, but induces a large consecration to God of all we have and are. So that prayer, thanksgiving and consecration are all linked together inseparably.

Gratitude and thanksgiving always looks back at the past though it may also take in the present. But prayer always looks to the future. Thanksgiving deals with things already received. Prayer deals with things desired, asked for and expected. Prayer turns to gratitude and praise when the things asked for have been granted by God.

As prayer brings things to us which beget gratitude and thanksgiving, so praise and gratitude promote prayer, and induce more praying and better praying.

Gratitude and thanksgiving forever stand opposed to all murmurings at God's dealings with us, and all complainings at our lot. Gratitude and murmuring never abide in the same heart at the same time. An unappreciative spirit has no standing beside gratitude and praise. And true prayer corrects complaining and promotes gratitude and thanksgiving. Dissatisfaction at one's lot, and a disposition to be discontented with things which come to us in the providence of God, are foes to gratitude and enemies to thanksgiving.

The murmurers are ungrateful people. Appreciative men and women have neither the time nor disposition to stop and complain. The bane of the wilderness-journey of the Israelites on their way to Canaan was their proneness to murmur and complain against God and Moses. For this, God was several times greatly grieved, and it took the strong praying of Moses to avert God's wrath because of these murmurings. The absence of gratitude left no room nor disposition for praise and thanksgiving, just as it is so always. But when these same Israelites were brought through the Red Sea dry shod, while their enemies were destroyed, there was a song of praise led by Miriam, the sister of Moses. One of the leading sins of these Israelites was forgetfulness of God and His mercies, and ingratitude of soul. This brought forth murmurings and lack of praise, as it always does.

When Paul wrote to the Colossians to let the word of Christ dwell in their hearts richly and to let the peace of God rule therein, he said to them, "and be ye thankful," and adds, "admonishing yourselves in psalms and hymns and spiritual songs, singing with grace in your hearts unto the Lord."

Further on, in writing to these same Christians, he joins prayer and thanksgiving together: "Continue in prayer, and watch in the same with thanksgiving."

And writing to the Thessalonians, he again joins them in union: "Rejoice evermore. Pray without ceasing. In everything give thanks, for this is the will of God concerning you."

> "We thank Thee, Lord of heaven and earth,
> Who hast preserved us from our birth;
> Redeemed us oft from death and dread,
> And with Thy gifts our table spread."

Wherever there is true prayer, there thanksgiving and gratitude stand hard by, ready to respond to the answer when it comes. For as prayer brings the answer, so the answer brings forth gratitude and praise. As prayer sets God to work, so answered prayer sets thanksgiving to work. Thanksgiving follows answered prayer just as day succeeds night.

True prayer and gratitude lead to full consecration, and consecration leads to more praying and better praying. A consecrated life is both a prayer-life and a thanksgiving life.

The spirit of praise was once the boast of the primitive Church. This spirit abode on the tabernacles of these early Christians, as a cloud of glory out of which God shined and spoke. It filled their temples with the perfume of costly, flaming incense. That this spirit of praise is sadly deficient in our present-day congregations must be evident to every careful observer. That it is a mighty force in projecting the Gospel, and its body of vital forces, must be equally evident. To restore the spirit of praise to our congregations should be one of the main points with every true pastor. The normal state of the Church is set forth in the declaration made to God in Psalm 65: "Praise waiteth for thee, O Lord, and unto thee shall the vow be performed."

Praise is so distinctly and definitely wedded to prayer, so inseparably joined, that they cannot be divorced. Praise is dependent on prayer for its full volume and its sweetest melody.

Singing is one method of praise, not the highest it is true, but it is the ordinary and usual form. The singing service in our churches has much to do with praise, for according to the character of the singing will be the genuineness or the measure of praise. The singing may be so directed as to have in it elements which deprave and debauch prayer. It may be so directed as to drive away everything like thanksgiving and praise. Much of modern singing in our churches is entirely foreign to anything like hearty, sincere praise to God.

The spirit of prayer and of true praise go hand in hand. Both are often entirely dissipated by the flippant, thoughtless, light singing in our congregations. Much of the singing lacks serious thought and is devoid of everything like a devotional spirit. Its lustiness and sparkle may not only dissipate all the essential features of worship, but may substitute the flesh for the spirit.

Giving thanks is the very life of prayer. It is its fragrance and music, its poetry and its crown. Prayer bringing the desired answer breaks out into praise and thanksgiving. So that whatever interferes with and injures the spirit of prayer necessarily hurts and dissipates the spirit of praise.

The heart must have in it the grace of prayer to sing the praise of God. Spiritual singing is not to be done by musical taste or talent, but by the grace of God in the heart. Nothing helps praise so mightily as a gracious revival of true religion in the Church. The conscious presence of God inspires song. The angels and the glorified ones in heaven do not need artistic precentors to lead them, nor do they care for paid choirs to chime in with their heavenly doxologies of praise and worship. They are not dependent on singing schools to teach them the notes and scale of singing. Their singing involuntarily breaks forth from the heart.

God is immediately present in the heavenly assemblies of the angels and the spirits of just men made perfect. His glorious presence creates the song, teaches the singing, and impregnates their notes of praise. It is so on earth. God's presence begets singing and thanksgiving, while the absence of God from our congregations is the death of song, or, which amounts to the same, makes the singing lifeless, cold and formal. His conscious presence in our churches would bring back the days of praise and would restore the full chorus of song.

Where grace abounds, song abounds. When God is in the heart, heaven is present and melody is there, and the lips overflow out of the abundance of the heart. This is as true in the private life of the believer as it is so in the congregations of the saints. The decay of singing, the dying down and out of the spirit of praise in song, means the decline of grace in the heart and the absence of God's presence from the people.

The main design of all singing is for God's ear and to attract His attention and to please Him. It is " to the Lord," for His glory, and to His honour. Certainly it is not for the glorification of the paid choir, to exalt the wonderful musical powers of the singers, nor is it to draw the people to the church, but it is for the glory of God and the good of the souls of the congregation. Alas! How far has the singing of choirs of churches of modern times departed from this idea! It is no surprise that there is no life, no power, no unction, no spirit, in much of the Church singing heard in this day. It is sacrilege for any but sanctified hearts and holy lips to direct the singing part of the service of God's house of prayer. Much of the singing in churches would do credit to the opera house, and might satisfy as mere entertainments, pleasing the ear, but as a part of real worship, having in it the spirit of praise and prayer, it is a fraud, an imposition on spiritually minded people, and entirely unacceptable to God. The cry should go out afresh, " Let all the people praise the Lord," for " it is good to sing praises unto our God; for it is pleasant; and praise is comely."

The music of praise, for there is real music of soul in praise, is too hopeful and happy to be denied. All these are in the " giving of thanks." In Philippians, prayer is called " requests." " Let your requests be made known unto God," which describes prayer as an asking for a gift, giving prominence to the thing asked for, making it emphatic, something to be given by God and received by us, and not something to be done by us. And all this is closely connected with gratitude to God, " with thanksgiving, let your requests be made known unto God."

God does much for us in answer to prayer, but we need from Him many gifts, and for them we are to make special prayer. According to our special needs, so must our praying be. We are to be special and particular and bring to the knowledge of God by prayer, supplication and thanksgiving, our particular requests, the things we need, the things we greatly desire. And with it all, accompanying all these requests, there must be thanksgiving.

It is indeed a pleasing thought that what we are called upon to do on earth, to praise and give thanks, the angels in heaven and the redeemed disembodied spirits of the saints are doing also. It is still further pleasing to contemplate the glorious hope that what God wants us to do on earth, we will be engaged in doing throughout an unending eternity. Praise and thanksgiving will be our blessed employment while we remain in heaven. Nor will we ever grow weary of this pleasing task.

Joseph Addison sets before us, in verse, this pleasing prospect:

> " Through every period of my life
>     Thy goodness I'll pursue;
> And after death, in distant worlds,
>     The pleasing theme renew.

> " Through all eternity to Thee
>     A grateful song I'll raise;
> But Oh! eternity's too short
>     To utter all Thy praise."

# V

## PRAYER AND TROUBLE

" 'He will.' It may not be today,
   That God Himself shall wipe our tears away,
   Nor, hope deferred, may it be yet tomorrow
   He'll take away our cup of earthly sorrow;
   But, precious promise, He has said He *will,*
   If we but trust Him fully—and be still.

"We, too, as He, may fall, and die unknown;
   And e'en the place we fell be all unshown,
   But eyes omniscient will mark the spot
   Till empires perish and the world's forgot.
   Then they who bore the yoke and drank the cup
   In fadeless glory shall the Lord raise up.
   God's word is ever good; His will is best:—
   The yoke, the heart all broken—and then rest."
               —CLAUDIUS L. CHILTON

TROUBLE and prayer are closely related to each other. Prayer is of great value to trouble. Trouble often drives men to God in prayer, while prayer is but the voice of men in trouble. There is great value in prayer in the time of trouble. Prayer often delivers out of trouble, and still oftener gives strength to bear trouble, ministers comfort in trouble, and begets patience in the midst of trouble. Wise is he in the day of trouble who knows his true source of strength and who fails not to pray.

Trouble belongs to the present state of man on earth. "Man that is born of a woman is of few days and full of trouble." Trouble is common to man. There is no exception in any age or clime or station. Rich and poor alike, the learned and the ignorant, one and all are partakers of this sad and painful inheritance of the fall of man. "There hath no temptation taken you but such as is common to man." The "day of trouble" dawns on every one at some time in his life. "The evil days come and the years draw nigh" when the heart feels its heavy pressure.

That is an entirely false view of life and shows supreme ignorance that expects nothing but sunshine and looks only for ease, pleasure and flowers. It is this class who are so sadly disappointed and surprised when trouble breaks into their lives. These are the ones who know not God, who know nothing of His disciplinary dealings with His people and who are prayerless.

What an infinite variety there is in the troubles of life! How diversified the experiences of men in the school of trouble! No two people have the same troubles under like environments. God deals with no two of His children in the same way. And as God varies His treatment of His children, so trouble is varied. God does not repeat Himself. He does not run in a rut. He has not one pattern for every child. Each trouble is proportioned to each child. Each one is dealt with according to his own peculiar case.

Trouble is God's servant, doing His will unless He is defeated in the execution of that will. Trouble is under the control of Almighty God, and is one of His most efficient agents in fulfilling His purposes and in perfecting His saints. God's hand is in every trouble which breaks into the lives of men. Not that He directly and arbitrarily orders every unpleasant experience of life. Not that He is personally responsible for every painful and afflicting thing which comes into the lives of His people. But no trouble is ever turned loose in this world and comes into the life of saint or sinner, but comes with Divine permission, and is allowed to exist and do its painful work with God's hand in it or on it, carrying out His gracious designs of redemption.

All things are under Divine control. Trouble is neither above God nor beyond His control. It is not something in life independent of God. No matter from what source it springs nor whence it arises, God is sufficiently wise and able to lay His hand upon it without assuming responsibility for its origin, and work it into His plans and purposes concerning the highest welfare of His saints. This is the explanation of that gracious statement in Romans, so often quoted, but the depth of whose meaning has rarely been sounded, " And we know that all things work together for good to them that love God."

Even the evils brought about by the forces of nature are His servants, carrying out His will and

fulfilling His designs. God even claims the locusts,
the cankerworm, the caterpillar are His servants,
"My great army," used by Him to correct His
people and discipline them.

Trouble belongs to the disciplinary part of the
moral government of God. This is a life of probation, where the human race is on probation. It
is a season of trial. Trouble is not penal in its
nature. It belongs to what the Scriptures call
"chastening." "Whom the Lord loveth he chasteneth, and scourgeth every son whom he receiveth."
Speaking accurately, punishment does not belong to
this life. Punishment for sin will take place in the
next world. God's dealings with people in this
world are of the nature of discipline. They are cor-
rective processes in His plans concerning man. It
is because of this that prayer comes in when trouble
arises. Prayer belongs to the discipline of life.

As trouble is not sinful in itself, neither is it the
evidence of sin. Good and bad alike experience
trouble. As the rain falls alike on the just and unjust, so drouth likewise comes to the righteous and
the wicked. Trouble is no evidence whatever of the
Divine displeasure. Scripture instances without
number disprove any such idea. Job is a case in
point, where God bore explicit testimony to his deep
piety, and yet God permitted Satan to afflict him
beyond any other man for wise and beneficent purposes. Trouble has no power in itself to interfere
with the relations of a saint to God. "Who shall

separate us from the love of Christ? Shall tribulation, or distress, or persecution, or famine, or
nakedness, or peril, or sword?"

Three words practically the same in the processes
of Divine discipline are found, temptation, trial and
trouble, and yet there is a difference between them.
Temptation is really a solicitation to evil arising
from the devil or born in the carnal nature of man.
Trial is testing. It is that which proves us, tests
us, and makes us stronger and better when we submit to the trial and work together with God in it.
"My brethren, count it all joy when ye fall into
divers temptations; knowing this, that the trying of
your faith worketh patience."

Peter speaks along the same line:

"Wherein ye greatly rejoice, now for a season, if
need be, ye are in heaviness through manifold temptations; that the trial of your faith being much more
precious than that of gold that perisheth, though it be
tried with fire, might be found unto praise, and honor
and glory at the appearing of Jesus Christ."

The third word is trouble itself, which covers all
the painful, sorrowing, and grievous events of life.
And yet temptations and trials might really become
troubles. So that all evil days in life might well be
classed under the head of the "time of trouble."
And such days of trouble are the lot of all men.
Enough to know that trouble, no matter from what
source it comes, becomes in God's hand His own

agent to accomplish His gracious work concerning those who submit patiently to Him, who recognise Him in prayer, and who work together with God.

Let us settle down at once to the idea that trouble arises not by chance, and neither occurs by what men call accident. " Although affliction cometh not forth of the dust, neither doth trouble spring out of the ground, yet man is born unto trouble as the sparks fly upward." Trouble naturally belongs to God's moral government, and is one of His invaluable agents in governing the world.

When we realise this, we can the better understand much that is recorded in the Scriptures, and can have a clearer conception of God's dealings with His ancient Israel. In God's dealings with them, we find what is called a history of Divine Providence, and providence always embraces trouble. No one can understand the story of Joseph and his old father Jacob unless he takes into the account trouble and its varied offices. God takes account of trouble when He urges His prophet Isaiah on this wise:

"Comfort ye, comfort ye my people, saith your God. Speak ye comfortably to Jerusalem, and cry unto her that her warfare is accomplished, that her iniquity is pardoned."

There is a distinct note of comfort in the Gospel for the praying saints of the Lord, and He is a wise scribe in Divine things who knows how to minister this comfort to the broken-hearted and sad ones of earth. Jesus Himself said to His sad disciples, "I will not leave you comfortless."

All the foregoing has been said that we may rightly appreciate the relationship of prayer to trouble. In the time of trouble, where does prayer come in? The Psalmist tells us: "Call upon me in the day of trouble; I will deliver thee, and thou shalt glorify me." Prayer is the most appropriate thing for a soul to do in the "time of trouble." Prayer recognises God in the day of trouble. "It is the Lord; let him do what seemeth him good." Prayer sees God's hand in trouble, and prays about it. Nothing more truly shows us our helplessness than when trouble comes. It brings the strong man low, it discloses our weakness, it brings a sense of helplessness. Blessed is he who knows how to turn to God in "the time of trouble." If trouble is of the Lord, then the most natural thing to do is to carry the trouble to the Lord, and seek grace and patience and submission. It is the time to inquire in the trouble, "Lord, what wilt thou have me to do?" How natural and reasonable for the soul, oppressed, broken, and bruised, to bow low at the footstool of mercy and seek the face of God? Where could a soul in trouble more likely find solace than in the closet?

Alas! trouble does not always drive men to God in prayer. Sad is the case of him who, when trouble bends his spirit down and grieves his heart, yet knows not whence the trouble comes nor knows how to pray about it. Blessed is the man who is driven by trouble to his knees in prayer!

> "Trials must and will befall;
>   But with humble faith to see
> Love inscribed upon them all—
>   This is happiness to me.
>
> "Trials make the promise sweet,
>   Trials give new life to prayer;
> Bring me to my Saviour's feet,
>   Lay me low, and keep me there."

Prayer in the time of trouble brings comfort, help, hope, and blessings, which, while not removing the trouble, enable the saint the better to bear it and to submit to the will of God. Prayer opens the eyes to see God's hand in trouble. Prayer does not interpret God's providences, but it does justify them and recognise God in them. Prayer enables us to see wise ends in trouble. Prayer in trouble drives us away from unbelief, saves us from doubt, and delivers from all vain and foolish questionings because of our painful experiences. Let us not lose sight of the tribute paid to Job when all his troubles came to the culminating point: "In all this Job sinned not, nor charged God foolishly."

Alas! for vain, ignorant men, without faith in God and knowing nothing of God's disciplinary processes in dealing with men, who charge God foolishly when troubles come, and who are tempted

to " curse God." How silly and vain are the complainings, the murmurings and the rebellion of men
in the time of trouble! What need to read again the
story of the Children of Israel in the wilderness!
And how useless is all our fretting, our worrying
over trouble, as if such unhappy doings on our part
could change things! "And which of you with
taking thought, can add to his stature one cubit?"
How much wiser, how much better, how much
easier to bear life's troubles when we take everything to God in prayer?

Trouble has wise ends for the praying ones, and
these find it so. Happy is he who, like the Psalmist,
finds that his troubles have been blessings in dis-
guise. "It is good for me that I have been afflicted, that I might learn thy statutes. I know, O
Lord, that thy judgments are right, and that thou
in faithfulness hast afflicted me."

" O who could bear life's stormy doom,
    Did not Thy wing of love
Come brightly wafting through the gloom
    Our peace branch from above.

" Then sorrow, touched by Thee, grows bright,
    With more than rapture's ray;
As darkness shows us worlds of light
    We never saw by day."

Of course it may be conceded that some troubles
are really imaginary. They have no existence other
than in the mind. Some are anticipated troubles,

which never arrive at our door. Others are past troubles, and there is much folly in worrying over them. Present troubles are the ones requiring attention and demanding prayer. "Sufficient unto the day is the evil thereof." Some troubles are self-originated. We are their authors. Some of these originate involuntarily with us, some arise from our ignorance, some come from our carelessness. All this can be readily admitted without breaking the force of the statement that they are the subjects of prayer, and should drive us to prayer. What father casts off his child who cries to him when the little one from its own carelessness has stumbled and fallen and hurt itself? Does not the cry of the child attract the ears of the father even though the child be to blame for the accident? "Whatever things ye desire" takes in every event of life, even though some events we are responsible for.

Some troubles are human in their origin. They arise from second causes. They originate with others and we are the sufferers. This is a world where often the innocent suffer the consequences of the acts of others. This is a part of life's incidents. Who has not at some time suffered at the hands of others? But even these are allowed to come in the order of God's providence, are permitted to break into our lives for beneficent ends, and may be prayed over. Why should we not carry our hurts, our wrongs and our privations, caused by the acts of others, to God in prayer? Are such things outside of the realm of prayer? Are they exceptions to the rule of prayer? Not at all. And God can and will lay His hand upon all such events in answer to prayer, and cause them to work for us "a far more exceeding and eternal weight of glory."

Nearly all of Paul's troubles arose from wicked and unreasonable men. Read the story as he gives it in II Corinthians 11:23-33.

So also some troubles are directly of Satanic origin. Quite all of Job's troubles were the offspring of the devil's scheme to break down Job's integrity, to make him charge God foolishly and to curse God. But are these not to be recognised in prayer? Are they to be excluded from God's disciplinary processes? Job did not do so. Hear him in those familiar words. "The Lord gave, and the Lord hath taken away. Blessed be the name of the Lord."

O what a comfort to see God in all of life's events! What a relief to a broken, sorrowing heart to see God's hand in sorrow! What a source of relief is prayer in unburdening the heart in grief!

"O Thou who driest the mourner's tear,
　　How dark this world would be,
If, when deceived and wounded here,
　　We could not fly to Thee?

"The friends who in our sunshine live,
　　When winter comes are flown,

And he who has but tears to give,
Must weep those tears alone.

"But Thou wilt heal the broken heart,
Which, like the plants that throw
Their fragrance from the wounded part,
Breathes sweetness out of woe."

But when we survey all the sources from which
trouble comes, it all resolves itself into two invaluable truths: First, that our troubles at last are of
the Lord. They come with His consent. He is in
all of them, and is interested in us when they press
and bruise us. And secondly, that our troubles, no
matter what the cause, whether of ourselves, or men
or devils, or even God Himself, we are warranted in
taking them to God in prayer, in praying over them,
and in seeking to get the greatest spiritual benefits
out of them.

Prayer in the time of trouble tends to bring the
spirit into perfect subjection to the will of God, to
cause the will to be conformed to God's will, and
saves from all murmurings over our lot, and delivers from everything like a rebellious heart or a
spirit critical of the Lord. Prayer sanctifies trouble to our highest good. Prayer so prepares the
heart that it softens under the disciplining hand of
God. Prayer places us where God can bring to us
the greatest good, spiritual and eternal. Prayer
allows God to freely work with us and in us in the
day of trouble. Prayer removes everything in the

way of trouble, bringing to us the sweetest, the
highest and greatest good. Prayer permits God's
servant, trouble, to accomplish its mission in us,
with us and for us.

The end of trouble is always good in the mind of
God. If trouble fails in its mission, it is either
because of prayerlessness or unbelief, or both. Being in harmony with God in the dispensations of
His providence, always makes trouble a blessing.
The good or evil of trouble is always determined by
the spirit in which it is received. Trouble proves a
blessing or a curse, just according as it is received
and treated by us. It either softens or hardens us.
It either draws us to prayer and to God or it drives
us from God and from the closet. Trouble hardened Pharaoh till finally it had no effect on him,
only to make him more desperate and to drive him
farther from God. The same sun softens the wax
and hardens the clay. The same sun melts the ice
and dries out the moisture from the earth.

As is the infinite variety of trouble, so also is
there infinite variety in the relations of prayer to
other things. How many are the things which are
the subject of prayer! It has to do with everything
which concerns us, with everybody with whom we
have to do, and has to do with all times. But especially does prayer have to do with trouble. "This
poor man cried and the Lord heard him, and saved
him out of all his troubles." O the blessedness, the
help, the comfort of prayer in the day of trouble!

And how marvelous the promises of God to us in the time of trouble!

" Because he hath set his love upon me, therefore will I deliver him; I will set him on high because he hath known my name. He shall call upon me, and I will answer him; I will be with him in trouble; I will deliver him and honor him."

> " If pain afflict, or wrongs oppress,
>     If cares distract, or fears dismay;
>   If guilt deject, if sin distress,
>     In every case, still watch and pray."

How rich in its sweetness, how far-reaching in the realm of trouble, and how cheering to faith, are the words of promise which God delivers to His believing, praying ones, by the mouth of Isaiah:

" But now, thus saith the Lord that created thee, O Jacob, and he that formed thee, O Israel, Fear not: for I have redeemed thee, I have called thee by thy name; thou art mine. When thou passest through the waters, I will be with thee; and through the rivers, they shall not overflow thee: when thou walkest through the fire, thou shalt not be burned: neither shall the flame kindle upon thee. . . . For I am the Lord thy God, the Holy One of Israel, thy Saviour."

# VI

## PRAYER AND TROUBLE (*Continued*)

"My first message for heavenly relief went singing over millions of miles of space in 1869, and brought relief to my troubled heart. But, thanks be to Him, I have received many delightful and helpful answers during the last fifty years. I would think the commerce of the skies had gone into bankruptcy if I did not hear frequently, since I have learned how to ask and how to receive."—REV. H. W. HODGE

IN the New Testament there are three words used which embrace trouble. These are tribulation, suffering and affliction, words differing somewhat, and yet each of them practically meaning trouble of some kind. Our Lord put His disciples on notice that they might expect tribulation in this life, teaching them that tribulation belonged to this world, and they could not hope to escape it; that they would not be carried through this life on flowery beds of ease. How hard to learn this plain and patent lesson! "In the world ye shall have tribulation; but be of good cheer; I have overcome the world." There is the encouragement. As He had overcome the world and its tribulations, so might they do the same.

Paul taught the same lesson throughout his ministry, when in confirming the souls of the brethren, and exhorting them to continue in the faith, he told them that "we must, through much tribulation, enter into the kingdom of God." He himself knew this by his own experience, for his pathway was anything but smooth and flowery.

He it is who uses the word "suffering" to describe the troubles of life, in that comforting passage in which he contrasts life's troubles with the final glory of heaven, which shall be the reward of all who patiently endure the ills of Divine Providence:

"For I reckon that the sufferings of this present time are not worthy to be compared with the glory which shall be revealed in us."

And he it is who speaks of the afflictions which come to the people of God in this world, and regards them as light as compared with the weight of glory awaiting all who are submissive, patient and faithful in all their troubles:

"For our light affliction, which is but for a moment, worketh for us a far more exceeding and eternal weight of glory."

But these present afflictions can work for us only as we co-operate with God in prayer. As God works through prayer, it is only through this means He can accomplish His highest ends for us. His Providence works with greatest effect with His

praying ones. These know the uses of trouble
and its gracious designs. The greatest value in
trouble comes to those who bow lowest before the
throne.

Paul, in urging patience in tribulation, connects
it directly with prayer, as if prayer alone would
place us where we could be patient when tribulation
comes. " Rejoicing in hope, patient in tribulation,
continuing instant in prayer." He here couples up
tribulation and prayer, showing their close relationship and the worth of prayer in begetting and cul-
turing patience in tribulation. In fact there can be
no patience exemplified when trouble comes, only as
it is secured through instant and continued prayer.
In the school of prayer is where patience is learned
and practiced.

Prayer brings us into that state of grace where
tribulation is not only endured, but where there is
under it a spirit of rejoicing. In showing the gracious benefits of justification, in Romans 5 : 3, Paul
says :

" And not only so, but we glory in tribulation also :
knowing that tribulation worketh patience ; and patience, experience ; and experience, hope ; and hope
maketh not ashamed ; because the love of God is shed
abroad in our hearts by the Holy Ghost which is given
unto us."

What a chain of graces are here set forth
as flowing from tribulation! What successive

steps to a high state of religious experience!
And what rich fruits result from even painful
tribulation!

To the same effect are the words of Peter in his
First Epistle, in his strong prayer for those Christians to whom he writes; thus showing that suffering and the highest state of grace are closely connected; and intimating that it is through suffering
we are to be brought to those higher regions of
Christian experience:

"But the God of all grace, who hath called us into
his eternal glory, by Christ Jesus, after that ye have
suffered awhile, make you perfect, stablish, strengthen
and settle you."

It is in the fires of suffering that God purifies
His saints and brings them to the highest things.
It is in the furnace their faith is tested, their patience is tried, and they are developed in all those
rich virtues which make up Christian character. It
is while they are passing through deep waters that
He shows how close He can come to His praying,
believing saints.

It takes faith of a high order and a Christian experience far above the average religion of this day,
to count it joy when we are called to pass through
tribulation. God's highest aim in dealing with His
people is in developing Christian character. He is
after begetting in us those rich virtues which belong to our Lord Jesus Christ. He is seeking to

make us like Himself. It is not so much work that
He wants in us. It is not greatness. It is the presence in us of patience, meekness, submission to the
Divine will, prayerfulness which brings everything
to Him. He seeks to beget His own image in us.
And trouble in some form tends to do this very
thing, for this is the end and aim of trouble. This
is its work. This is the task it is called to perform.
It is not a chance incident in life, but has a design
in view, just as it has an All-wise Designer back of
it, who makes trouble His agent to bring forth the
largest results.

The writer of the Epistle to the Hebrews gives
us a perfect directory of trouble, comprehensive,
clear and worth while to be studied. Here is " chastisement," another word for trouble, coming from
a Father's hand, showing God is in all the sad and
afflictive events of life. Here is its nature and its
gracious design. It is not punishment in the accu-
rate meaning of that word, but the means God em-
ploys to correct and discipline His children in
dealing with them on earth. Then we have the fact
of the evidence of being His people, namely, the
presence of chastisement. The ultimate end is that
we " may be partakers of his holiness," which is but
another way of saying that all this disciplinary
process is to the end that God may make us like
Himself. What an encouragement, too, that, chastisement is no evidence of anger or displeasure on
God's part, but is the strong proof of His love. Let

us read the entire directory on this important
subject:

"And ye have forgotten the exhortation which
speaketh unto you as unto children, My son, despise
not thou the chastening of the Lord, nor faint when
thou art rebuked of him: For whom the Lord loveth
he chasteneth, and scourgeth every son whom he receiveth. If ye endure chastening, God dealeth with
you as with sons; for what son is he whom the father
chasteneth not? But if ye are without chastisement,
whereof all are partakers, then are ye bastards and
not sons.

"Furthermore, we have had fathers of our flesh
which corrected us, and we gave them reverence:
shall we not much rather be in subjection to the
Father of spirits and live? For they verily for a few
days chastened us after their own pleasure; but he
for our profit, that we might be partakers of his holiness. Now no chastening for the present seemeth to
be joyous, but grievous; nevertheless, afterward it
yieldeth the peaceable fruit of righteousness to them
which are exercised thereby."

Just as prayer is wide in its range, taking in
everything, so trouble is infinitely varied in its uses
and designs. It takes trouble sometimes to arrest
attention, to stop men in the busy rush of life, and
to awaken them to a sense of their helplessness
and their need and sinfulness. Not till King
Manasseh was bound with thorns and carried
away into a foreign land and got into deep trouble, was he awakened and brought back to God. It

was then he humbled himself and began to call upon God.

The Prodigal Son was independent and self-sufficient when in prosperity, but when money and friends departed, and he began to be in want, then it was he " came to himself," and decided to return to his father's house, with prayer and confession on his lips. Many a man who has forgotten God has been arrested, caused to consider his ways, and brought to remember God and pray by trouble. Blessed is trouble when it accomplishes this in men!

It is for this among other reasons that Job says:

" Behold, happy is the man whom God correcteth. Therefore, despise not thou the chastening of the Almighty. For he maketh sore, and bindeth up; he woundeth, and his hands maketh whole. He shall deliver thee in six troubles; yea, in seven there shall no evil touch thee."

One thing more might be named. Trouble makes earth undesirable and causes heaven to loom up large in the horizon of hope. There is a world where trouble never comes. But the path of tribulation leads to that world. Those who are there went there through tribulation. What a world set before our longing eyes which appeals to our hopes, as sorrows like a cyclone sweep over us! Hear John, as he talks about it and those who are there:

" What are these which are arrayed in white robes?

and whence came they? . . . And he said to me,
These are they which came out of great tribulation,
and have washed their robes and made them white
in the blood of the Lamb . . . And God shall wipe
away all tears from their eyes."

> " There I shall bathe my weary soul,
>     In seas of heavenly rest,
> And not a wave of trouble roll,
>     Across my peaceful breast."

Oh, children of God, ye who have suffered, who
have been sorely tried, whose sad experiences have
often brought broken spirits and bleeding hearts,
cheer up! God is in all your troubles, and He will
see that all shall " work together for good," if you
will but be patient, submissive and prayerful.

# VII

## PRAYER AND GOD'S WORK

"If Jacob's desire had been given him in time for him to get a good night's sleep he might never have become the prince of prayers we know today. If Hannah's prayer for a son had been answered at the time she set for herself, the nation might never have known the mighty man of God it found in Samuel. Hannah wanted only a son, but God wanted more. He wanted a prophet, and a saviour, and a ruler for His people. Some one said that 'God had to get a woman before He could get a man.' This woman He got in Hannah precisely by those weeks and months and years there came a woman with a vision like God's, with tempered soul and gentle spirit and a seasoned will, prepared to be the kind of a mother for the kind of a man God knew the nation needed."—W. E. BIEDERWOLF

GOD has a great work on hand in this world. This work is involved in the plan of salvation. It embraces redemption and providence. God is governing this world, with its intelligent beings, for His own glory and for their good. What, then, is God's work in this world? Rather what is the end He seeks in His great work? It is nothing short of holiness of heart and life in the children of fallen Adam. Man is a fallen creature, born with an evil nature, with an evil bent, unholy propensities, sinful desires, wicked inclinations. Man is unholy by nature, born so. "They go astray as soon as they be born, speaking lies."

God's entire plan is to take hold of fallen man and to seek to change him and make him holy. God's work is to make holy men out of unholy men. This is the very end of Christ coming into the world:

" For this purpose was the Son of God manifested that he might destroy the works of the devil."

God is holy in nature and in all His ways, and He wants to make man like Himself.

" As he who hath called you is holy, so be ye holy in all manner of conversation; because it is written, Be ye holy, for I am holy."

This is being Christlike. This is following Jesus Christ. This is the aim of all Christian effort. This is the earnest, heartfelt desire of every truly regenerated soul. This is what is to be constantly and earnestly prayed for. It is that we may be made holy. Not that we must make ourselves holy, but we must be cleansed from all sin by the precious atoning blood of Christ, and be made holy by the direct agency of the Holy Spirit. Not that we are to *do* holy, but rather to *be* holy. Being must precede doing. First be, then do. First, obtain a holy heart, then live a holy life. And for this high and gracious end God has made the most ample provisions in the atoning work of our Lord and through the agency of the Holy Spirit.

The work of God in the world is the implantation, the growth and the perfection of holiness in His people. Keep this ever in mind. But we might ask just now, Is this work advancing in the Church? Are men and women being made holy? Is the present-day Church engaged in the business of making holy men and women? This is not a vain and speculative question. It is practical, pertinent and all important.

The present-day Church has vast machinery. Her activities are great, and her material prosperity is unparalleled. The name of religion is widely-spread and well-known. Much money comes into the Lord's treasury and is paid out. But here is the question: Does the work of holiness keep pace with all this? Is the burden of the prayers of Church people to be made holy? Are our preachers really holy men? Or to go back a little further, are they hungering and thirsting after righteousness, desiring the sincere milk of the Word that they may grow thereby? Are they really seeking to be holy men? Of course men of intelligence are greatly needed in the pulpit, but prior to that, and primary to it, is the fact that we need holy men to stand before dying men and proclaim the salvation of God to them.

Ministers, like laymen, and no more so than laymen, must be holy men in life, in conversation and in temper. They must be examples to the flock of God in all things. By their lives they are to preach as well as to speak. Men in the pulpit are needed who are spotless in life, circumspect in behaviour, " without rebuke and blameless in the midst of a crooked and perverse nation, among whom they are to shine in the world." Are our preachers of this type of men? We are simply asking the question. Let the reader make up his own judgment. Is the work of holiness making progress among our preachers?

Again let us ask: Are our leading laymen examples of holiness? Are they seeking holiness of heart and life? Are they praying men, ever praying that God would fashion them according to His pattern of holiness? Are their business ways without stain of sin, and their gains free from the taint of wrong-doing? Have they the foundation of solid honesty, and does uprightness bring them into elevation and influence? Does business integrity and probity run parallel with religious activity, and with churchly observance?

Then, while we are pursuing our investigation, seeking light as to whether the work of God among His people is making progress, let us ask further as to our women. Are the leading women of our churches dead to the fashions of this world, separated from the world, not conformed to the world's maxims and customs? Are they in behaviour as becometh holiness, teaching the young women by word and life the lessons of soberness, obedience, and home-keeping? Are our women noted for their praying habits? Are they patterns of prayer?

How searching are all these questions? And will any one dare say they are impertinent and out of place? If God's work be to make men and women holy, and He has made ample provisions in the law of prayer of doing this very thing, why should it be thought impertinent and useless to propound such personal and pointed questions as these? They have to do directly with the work and with its progress and its perfection. They go to the very seat of the disease. They hit the spot.

We might as well face the situation first as last. There is no use to shut our eyes to real facts. If the Church does not do this sort of work—if the Church does not advance its members in holiness of heart and life—then all our show of activities and all our display of Church work are a delusion and a snare.

But let us ask as to another large and important class of people in our churches. They are the hope of the future Church. To them all eyes are turned. Are our young men and women growing in sober-mindedness and reverence, and in all those graces which have their root in the renewed heart, which mark solid and permanent advance in the Divine life? If we are not growing in holiness, then we are doing nothing religious nor abiding.

Material prosperity is not the infallible sign of spiritual prosperity. The former may exist while the latter is significantly absent. Material prosperity may easily blind the eyes of Church leaders, so much so that they will make it a substitute for spiritual prosperity. How great the need to watch at that point! Prosperity in money matters does not signify growth in holiness. The seasons of material prosperity are rarely seasons of spiritual advance, either to the individual or to the Church. It is so easy to lose sight of God when goods increase. It so easy to lean on human agencies and cease praying and relying upon God when material prosperity comes to the Church.

If it be contended that the work of God is progressing, and that we are growing in holiness, then some perplexing questions arise which will be hard to answer. If the Church is making advances on the lines of deep spirituality—if we are a praying people, noted for our prayer habits—if our people are hungering after holiness—then let us ask, why do we now have so few mighty outpourings of the Holy Spirit on our chief churches and our principal appointments? Why is it that so few of our revivals spring from the life of the pastor, who is noted for his deep spirituality, or the life of our church? Is the Lord's hand shortened that He cannot save? Is His ear heavy that He cannot hear? Why is it that in order to have so-called revivals, we must have outside pressure, by the reputation and sensation of some renowned evangelist? This is largely true in our larger charges and with our leading men. Why is it that the pastor is not sufficiently spiritual, holy and in communion with God, that he cannot hold his own revival services, and have large outpourings of the Holy Spirit on the Church, the community and upon himself? There can be but one solution for all this state of things. We have cultivated other things to the neglect of the work of holiness. We have permitted our minds to be pre-occupied with material things in the Church. Unfortunately, whether designedly or not, we have substituted the external for the internal. We have put that which is seen to the front and shut out that which is unseen. It is all too true as to the Church, that we are much further advanced in material matters than in matters spiritual.

But the cause of this sad state of things may be traced further back. It is largely due to the decay of prayer. For with the decline of the work of holiness there has come the decline of the business of praying. As praying and holiness go together, so the decline of one, means the decay of the other. Excuse it if we may, justify the present state of things if we will, yet it is all too patent that the emphasis in the work of the present-day Church is not put on prayer. And just as this has occurred, the emphasis has been taken from the great work of God set on foot in the atonement, holiness of heart and life. The Church is not turning out praying men and women, because the Church is not intently engaged in the one great work of holiness.

At one time, John Wesley saw that there was a perceptible decline in the work of holiness, and he stopped short to inquire into the cause, and if we are as honest and spiritual as he was, we will now see the same causes operating to stay God's work among us. In a letter to his brother, Charles, at one time, he comes directly to the point, and makes short, incisive work of it. Here is how he begins his letter:

" What has hindered the work? I want to consider this. And must we not first say, we are the chief. If we were more holy in heart and life, thoroughly devoted to God, would not all the preachers catch fire, and carry it with them, throughout the land?

" Is not the next hindrance the littleness of grace (rather than of gifts) in a considerable part of our preachers? They have not the whole mind that was in Christ. They do not steadily walk as He walked. And, therefore, the hand of the Lord is stayed, though not altogether; though He does work still. But it is not in such a degree as He surely would, were they holy as He that hath sent them is holy.

" Is not the third hindrance the littleness of grace in the generality of our people? Therefore, they pray little, and with little fervency for a general blessing. And, therefore, their prayer has little power with God. It does not, as once, shut and open heaven.

" Add to this, that as there is much of the spirit of the world in their hearts, so there is much conformity to the world in their lives. They ought to be bright and shining lights, but they neither burn nor shine. They are not true to the rules they profess to observe. They are not holy in all manner of conversation. Nay, many of them are salt that has lost its savour, the little savour they once had. Wherewith then shall the rest of the land be seasoned? What wonder that their neighbours are as unholy as ever?"

He strikes the spot. He hits the centre. He grades the cause. He freely confesses that he and Charles are the first cause, in this decline of holiness. The chief ones occupy positions of responsibility. As they go, so goes the Church. They give colour to the Church. They largely determine its character and its work. What holiness should mark these chief men? What zeal should ever characterise them? What prayerfulness should be seen in them! How influential they ought to be with God! If the head be weak, then the whole body will feel the stroke.

The pastors come next in his catalogue. When the chief shepherds and those who are under them, the immediate pastors, stay their advance in holiness, the panic will reach to the end of the line. As are the pastors, so will the poeple be as a rule. If the pastors are prayerless, then will the people follow in their footsteps. If the preacher be silent upon the work of holiness, then will there be no hungering and thirsting after holiness in the laymen. If the preacher be careless about obtaining the highest and best God has for him in religious experience, then will the people take after him.

One statement of Wesley needs to be repeated with emphasis. The littleness of grace, rather than

the smallness of gifts,—this is largely the case with
the preachers.  It may be stated as an axiom: That
the work of God fails as a general rule, more for
the lack of grace, than for the want of gifts.  It is
more than this.  It is more than this, for a full sup-
ply of grace brings an increase of gifts.  It may be
repeated that small results, a low experience, a low
religious life, and pointless, powerless preaching
always flow from a lack of grace.  And a lack of
grace flows from a lack of praying.  Great grace
comes from great praying.

> " What is our calling's glorious hope
>         But inward holiness?
> For this to Jesus I look up,
>     I calmly wait for this.

> " I wait till He shall touch me clean,
>         Shall life and power impart;
> Give me the faith that casts out sin,
>     And purifies the heart."

In carrying on His great work in the world, God
works through human agents.  He works through
His Church collectively and through His people in-
dividually.  In order that they may be effective
agents, they must be " vessels unto honour, sanctified, and meet for the Master's use, and prepared
unto every good work."  God works most effect-
ively through holy men.  His work makes progress
in the hands of praying men.  Peter tells us that
husbands who might not be reached by the Word of

God, might be won by the conversation of their wives. It is those who are " blameless and harmless, the sons of God," who can hold forth the word of life " in the midst of a crooked and perverse nation."

The world judges religion not by what the Bible says, but by how Christians live. Christians are the Bible which sinners read. These are the epistles to be read of all men. " By their fruits ye shall know them." The emphasis, then, is to be placed upon holiness of life. But unfortunately in the present-day Church, emphasis has been placed elsewhere. In selecting Church workers and choosing ecclesiastical officers, the quality of holiness is not considered. The praying fitness seems not to be taken into account, when it was just otherwise in all of God's movements and in all of His plans. He looked for holy men, those noted for their praying habits. Prayer leaders are scarce. Prayer conduct is not counted as the highest qualification for offices in the Church.

We cannot wonder that so little is accomplished in the great work in the world which God has in hand. The fact is that it is surprising so much has been done with such feeble, defective agents. " Holiness to the Lord " needs again to be written on the banners of the Church. Once more it needs to be sounded out in the ears of modern Christians. " Follow peace with all men, and holiness, without which no man shall see the Lord."

Let it be iterated and reiterated that this is the Divine standard of religion. Nothing short of this will satisfy the Divine requirement. O the danger of deception at this point! How near one can come to being right and yet be wrong! Some men can come very near to pronouncing the test word, " Shibboleth," but they miss it. " Many will say unto me, Lord, Lord, in that day," says Jesus Christ, but He further states that then will He say unto them, " I never knew you; depart from me, ye that work iniquity."

Men can do many good things and yet not be holy in heart and righteous in conduct. They can do many good things and lack that spiritual quality of heart called holiness. How great the need of hearing the words of Paul guarding us against self-deception in the great work of personal salvation:

" Be not deceived; God is not mocked: for whatsoever a man soweth, that shall he also reap."

" O may I still from sin depart;
   A wise and understanding heart,
      Jesus, to me to be given;
   And let me through thy Spirit know
   To glorify my God below,
      And find my way to heaven."

# VIII

## PRAYER AND CONSECRATION

"Eudamidas, a citizen of Corinth, died in poverty; but having two wealthy friends, Arctæus and Carixenus, left the following testament: In virtue of my last will, I bequeath to Arctæus my mother and to Charixenus my daughter to be taken home to their houses and supported for the remainder of their lives. This testament occasioned much mirth and laughter. The two legatees were pleased and affectionately executed the will. If heathens trusted each other, why should not I cherish a far greater confidence in my beloved Master, Jesus? I hereby, therefore, nominate Him my sole heir, consigning to Him my soul and my children and sisters, that He may adopt, protect, and provide for them by His mighty power unto salvation. The whole residue of the estate shall be entrusted to His holy counsel."—GOTTHOLD

WHEN we study the many-sidedness of prayer, we are surprised at the number of things with which it is connected. There is no phase of human life which it does not affect, and it has to do with everything affecting human salvation. Prayer and consecration are closely related. Prayer leads up to, and governs consecration. Prayer is precedent to consecration, accompanies it, and is a direct result of it. Much goes under the name of consecration which has no consecration in it. Much consecration of the present day is defective, superficial and spurious, worth nothing so far as the office and ends of consecration are concerned. Popular consecration is sadly at fault because it has little or no prayer in it. No consecration is worth a thought which is not the direct fruit of much praying, and which fails to bring one into a life of prayer. Prayer is the one thing prominent in a consecrated life.

Consecration is much more than a life of so-called service. It is a life of personal holiness, first of all. It is that which brings spiritual power into the heart and enlivens the entire inner man. It is a life which ever recognises God, and a life given up to true prayer.

Full consecration is the highest type of a Christian life. It is the one Divine standard of experience, of living and of service. It is the one thing at which the believer should aim. Nothing short of entire consecration must satisfy him.

Never is he to be contented till he is fully, entirely the Lord's by his own consent. His praying naturally and in luntarily leads up to this one act of his.

Consecration is the voluntary set dedication of one's self to God, an offering definitely made, and made without any reservation whatever. It is the setting apart of all we are, all we have, and all we expect to have or be, to God first of all. It is not so much the giving of ourselves to the Church, or the mere engaging in some one line of Church work. Almighty God is in view and He is the end of all consecration. It is a separation of one's self to God, a devotement of all that he is and has to a sacred use. Some things may be devoted to a special purpose, but it is not consecration in the true sense. Consecration has a sacred nature. It is devoted to holy ends. It is the voluntary putting of one's self in God's hands to be used sacredly, holily, with sanctifying ends in view.

Consecration is not so much the setting one's self apart from sinful things and wicked ends, but rather it is the separation from worldly, secular and even legitimate things, if they come in conflict with God's plans, to holy uses. It is the devoting of all we have to God for His own specific use. It is a separation from things questionable, or even legitimate, when the choice is to be made between the things of this life and the claims of God.

The consecration which meets God's demands and which He accepts is to be full, complete, with no mental reservation, with nothing withheld. It cannot be partial, any more than a whole burnt offering in Old Testament times could have been partial. The whole animal had to be offered in sacrifice. To reserve any part of the animal would have seriously vitiated the offering. So to make a half-hearted, partial consecration is to make no consecration at all, and is to fail utterly in securing the Divine acceptance. It involves our whole being, all we have and all that we are. Everything is definitely and voluntarily placed in God's hands for His supreme use.

Consecration is not all there is in holiness. Many make serious mistakes at this point. Consecration makes us relatively holy. We are holy only in the sense that we are now closely related to God, in which we were not related heretofore. Consecration is the human side of holiness. In this sense, it is self-sanctification, and only in this sense. Sanctification or holiness in its truest and highest sense is Divine, the act of the Holy Spirit working in the heart, making it clean and putting therein in a higher degree the fruits of the Spirit.

This distinction is clearly set forth and kept in view by Moses in "Leviticus," wherein he shows the human and the Divine side of sanctification or holiness:

" Sanctify yourselves, therefore, and be ye holy, for I am the Lord your God. And ye shall keep my statutes and do them; I am the Lord which sanctify you."

Here we are to sanctify ourselves, and then in the next word we are taught that it is the Lord which sanctifies us. God does not consecrate us to His service. We do not sanctify ourselves in this highest sense. Here is the two-fold meaning of sanctification, and a distinction which needs to be always kept in mind.

Consecration being the intelligent, voluntary act of the believer, this act is the direct result of praying. No prayerless man ever conceives the idea of a full consecration. Prayerlessness and consecration have nothing whatever in common. A life of prayer naturally leads up to full consecration. It leads nowhere else. In fact, a life of prayer is satisfied with nothing else but an entire dedication of one's self to God. Consecration recognises fully God's ownership to us. It cheerfully assents to the truth set forth by Paul:

"Ye are not your own. For ye are bought with a price. Therefore, glorify God in your body and spirit, which are God's."

And true praying leads that way. It cannot reach any other destination. It is bound to run into this depot. This is its natural result. This is the sort of work which praying turns out. Praying makes consecrated people. It cannot make any other sort. It drives to this end. It aims at this very purpose.

As prayer leads up to and brings forth full consecration, so prayer entirely impregnates a consecrated life. The prayer life and the consecrated life are intimate companions. They are Siamese twins, inseparable. Prayer enters into every phase of a consecrated life. A prayerless life which claims consecration is a misnomer, false, counterfeit.

Consecration is really the setting apart of one's self to a life of prayer. It means not only to pray, but to pray habitually, and to pray more effectually. It is the consecrated man who accomplishes most by His praying. God must hear the man wholly given up to God. God cannot deny the requests of him

who has renounced all claims to himself, and who
has wholly dedicated himself to God and His service.   This act of the consecrated man puts him " on
praying ground and pleading terms " with God.   It
puts Him in reach of God in prayer.   It places him
where he can get hold of God, and where he can
influence God to do things which He would not
otherwise do.   Consecration brings answers to
prayer.   God can depend upon consecrated men.
God can afford to commit Himself in prayer to
those who have fully committed themselves to God.
He who gives all to God will get all from God.
Having given all to God, he can claim all that
God has for him.

As prayer is the condition of full consecration, so
prayer is the habit, the rule, of him who has dedicated himself wholly to God.   Prayer is becoming
in the consecrated life.   Prayer is no strange thing
in such a life.   There is a peculiar affinity between
prayer and consecration, for both recognise God,
both submit to God, and both have their aim and
end in God.   Prayer is part and parcel of the consecrated life.   Prayer is the constant, the inseparable,
the intimate companion of consecration.   They
walk and talk together.

There is much talk today of consecration, and
many are termed consecrated people who know not
the alphabet of it.   Much modern consecration falls
far below the Scripture standard.   There is really
no real consecration in it.   Just as there is much

praying without any real prayer in it, so there is much so-called consecration current, today, in the Church which has no real consecration in it. Much passes for consecration in the Church which receives the praise and plaudits of superficial, formal professors, but which is wide of the mark. There is much hurrying to and fro, here and there, much fuss and feathers, much going about and doing many things, and those who busy themselves after this fashion are called consecrated men and women. The central trouble with all this false consecration is that there is no prayer in it, nor is it in any sense the direct result of praying. People can do many excellent and commendable things in the Church and be utter strangers to a life of consecration, just as they can do many things and be prayerless.

Here is the true test of consecration. It is a life of prayer. Unless prayer be pre-eminent, unless prayer is to the front, the consecration is faulty, deceptive, falsely named. Does he pray? That is the test-question of every so-called consecrated man. Is he a man of prayer? No consecration is worth a thought if it be devoid of prayer. Yea, more—if it be not pre-eminently and primarily a life of prayer.

God wants consecrated men because they can pray and will pray. He can use consecrated men because He can use praying men. As prayerless men are in His way, hinder Him, and prevent the success of His cause, so likewise unconsecrated men are useless to Him, and hinder Him in carrying out His

gracious plans, and in executing His noble purposes
in redemption.  God wants consecrated men because He wants praying men.  Consecration and
prayer meet in the same man.  Prayer is the tool
with which the consecrated man works.  Consecrated men are the agents through whom prayer
works.  Prayer helps the consecrated man in main-
taining his attitude of consecration, keeps him alive
to God, and aids him in doing the work to which
he is called and to which he has given himself.
Consecration helps to effectual praying.  Consecration enables one to get the most out of his praying.

> " Let Him to whom we now belong
>     His sovereign right assert;
> And take up every thankful song,
>     And every loving heart.
>
> " He justly claims us for His own,
>     Who bought us with a price;
> The Christian lives to Christ alone,
>     To Christ alone he dies."

We must insist upon it that the prime purpose of
consecration is not service in the ordinary sense of
that word.  Service in the minds of not a few
means nothing more than engaging in some of the
many forms of modern Church activities.  There
are a multitude of such activities, enough to engage
the time and mind of any one, yea, even more than
enough.  Some of these may be good, others not so
good.  The present-day Church is filled with ma-

chinery, organisations, committees and societies, so
much so that the power it has is altogether insuf-
ficient to run the machinery, or to furnish life
sufficient to do all this external work.  Consecration
has a much higher and nobler end than merely to
expend itself in these external things.

Consecration aims at the right sort of service—
the Scriptural kind.  It seeks to serve God, but in
entirely a different sphere than that which is in the
minds of present-day Church leaders and workers.
The very first sort of service mentioned by Zach-
ariah, father of John the Baptist, in his wonderful
prophecy and statement in Luke 1:74, was thus:

"That he would grant unto us, that we, being delivered out of the hand of our enemies, might serve
him without fear, in holiness and righteousness, all
the days of our life."

Here we have the idea of "serving God in holiness and righteousness all the days of our life."

And the same kind of service is mentioned in
Luke's strong tribute to the father and mother of
John the Baptist before the latter's birth:

"And they were both righteous before God, walking in all the commandments and ordinances of the
Lord blameless."

And Paul, in writing to the Philippians, strikes
the same keynote in putting the emphasis on blame-
lessness of life:

" Do all things without murmurings and disputings, that ye may be blameless and harmless, the sons of God without rebuke, in the midst of a crooked and perverse nation, among whom ye shine as lights in the world; holding forth the word of life."

We must mention a truth which is strangely overlooked in these days by what are called personal workers, that in the Epistles of Paul and others, it is not what are called Church activities which are brought to the front, but rather the personal life. It is good behaviour, righteous conduct, holy living, godly conversation, right tempers—things which belong primarily to the personal life in religion. Everywhere this is emphasised, put in the forefront, made much of and insisted on. Religion first of all puts one to living right. Religion shows itself in the life. Thus is religion to prove its reality, its sincerity and its Divinity.

> " So let our lips and lives express
> The holy Gospel we profess;
> So let our works and virtues shine
> To prove the doctrine all Divine.

> " Thus shall we best proclaim abroad
> The honors of our Saviour God;
> When the salvation reigns within
> And grace subdues the power of sin."

The first great end of consecration is holiness of heart and of life. It is to glorify God, and this can be done in no more effectual way than by a holy life flowing from a heart cleansed from all sin. The great burden of heart pressed on every one who bceomes a Christian lies right here. This he is to ever keep in mind, and to further this kind of life and this kind of heart, he is to watch, to pray, and to bend all his diligence in using all the means of grace. He who is truly and fully consecrated, lives a holy life. He seeks after holiness of heart. Is not satisfied without it. For this very purpose he consecrates himself to God. He gives himself entirely over to God in order to be holy in heart and in life.

As holiness of heart and of life is thoroughly impregnated with prayer, so consecration and prayer are closely allied in personal religion. It takes prayer to bring one into such a consecrated life of holiness to the Lord, and it takes prayer to maintain such a life. Without much prayer, such a life of holiness will break down. Holy people are praying people. Holiness of heart and life puts people to praying. Consecration puts people to praying in earnest.

Prayerless people are strangers to anything like holiness of heart and cleanness of heart. Those who are unfamiliar with the closet are not at all interested in consecration and holiness. Holiness thrives in the place of secret prayer. The environments of the closet of prayer are favourable to its being and its culture. In the closet holiness is found. Consecration brings one into holiness of heart, and prayer stands hard by when it is done.

The spirit of consecration is the spirit of prayer. The law of consecration is the law of prayer. Both laws work in perfect harmony without the slightest jar or discord. Consecration is the practical expression of true prayer. People who are consecrated are known by their praying habits. Consecration thus expresses itself in prayer. He who is not interested in prayer has no interest in consecration. Prayer creates an interest in consecration, then prayer brings one into a state of heart where consecration is a subject of delight, bringing joy of heart, satisfaction of soul, contentment of spirit. The consecrated soul is the happiest soul. There is no friction whatever between him who is fully given over to God and God's will. There is perfect harmony between the will of such a man and God, and His will. And the two wills being in perfect accord, this brings rest of soul, absence of friction, and the presence of perfect peace.

" Lord, in the strength of grace,
    With a glad heart and free,
Myself, my residue of days,
    I consecrate to Thee.

" Thy ransomed servant, I
    Restore to Thee Thy own;
And from this moment, live or die,
    To serve my God alone."

# IX

## PRAYER AND A DEFINITE RELIGIOUS STANDARD

"The Angel Gabriel described Him as 'that holy thing' before He was born. As He was, so are we, in our measure, in this world."—Dr. Alexander Whyte

MUCH of the feebleness, barrenness and paucity of religion results from the failure to have a Scriptural and reasonable standard in religion, by which to shape character and measure results; and this largely results from the omission of prayer or the failure to put prayer in the standard. We cannot possibly mark our advances in religion if there is no point to which we are definitely advancing. Always there must be something definite before the mind's eye at which we are aiming and to which we are driving. We cannot contrast shapeliness with unshapeliness if there be no pattern after which to model. Neither can there be inspiration if there be no high end to stimulate us.

Many Christians are disjointed and aimless because they have no pattern before them after which conduct and character are to be shaped. They just move on aimlessly, their minds in a cloudy state,

93

no pattern in view, no point in sight, no standard after which they are striving. There is no standard by which to value and gauge their efforts. No magnet is there to fill their eyes, quicken their steps, and to draw them and keep them steady.

All this vague idea of religion grows out of loose notions about prayer. That which helps to make the standard of religion clear and definite is prayer. That which aids in placing that standard high is prayer. The praying ones are those who have something definite in view. In fact prayer itself is a very definite thing, aims at something specific, and has a mark at which it aims. Prayer aims at the most definite, the highest and the sweetest religious experience. The praying ones want all that God has in store for them. They are not satisfied with anything like a low religious life, superficial, vague and indefinite. The praying ones are not only after a " deeper work of grace," but want the very deepest work of grace possible and promised. They are not after being saved from some sin, but saved from all sin, both inward and outward. They are after not only deliverance from sinning, but from sin itself, from its being, its power and its pollution. They are after holiness of heart and life.

Prayer believes in, and seeks for the very highest religious life set before us in the Word of God. Prayer is the condition of that life. Prayer points out the only pathway to such a life. The standard of a religious life is the standard of prayer. Prayer is so vital, so essential, so far-reaching, that it enters into all religion, and sets the standard clear and definite before the eye. The degree of our estimate of prayer fixes our ideas of the standard of a religious life. The standard of Bible religion is the standard of prayer. The more there is of prayer in the life, the more definite and the higher our notions of religion.

The Scriptures alone make the standard of life and experience. When we make our own standard, there is delusion and falsity for our desires, convenience and pleasure form the rule, and that is always a fleshly and a low rule. From it, all the fundamental principles of a Christly religion are left out. Whatever standard of religion which makes in it provision for the flesh, is unscriptural and hurtful.

Nor will it do to leave it to others to fix the standard of religion for us. When we allow others to make our standard of religion, it is generally deficient because in imitation, defects are transferred to the imitator more readily than virtues, and a second edition of a man is marred by its defects.

The most serious damage in thus determining what religion is by what others say, is in allowing current opinion, the contagion of example, the grade of religion current among us, to shape our religious opinions and characters. Adoniram Judson once wrote to a friend, " Let me beg you, not to rest contented with the commonplace religion that is now so prevalent."

Commonplace religion is pleasing to flesh and blood. There is no self-denial in it, no cross bearing, no self-crucifixion. It is good enough for our neighbours. Why should we be singular and straight-laced? Others are living on a low plane, on a compromising level, living as the world lives. Why should we be peculiar, zealous of good works? Why should we fight to win heaven while so many are sailing there on " flowery beds of ease "? Are the easy-going, careless, sauntering crowd, living prayerless lives, going to heaven? Is heaven a fit place for non-praying, loose living, ease loving people? That is the supreme question.

Paul gives the following caution about making for ourselves the jolly, pleasure-seeking religious company all about us the standard of our measurement:

" For we dare not make ourselves of the number, or compare ourselves with some that commend themselves; but they, measuring themselves by themselves, and comparing themselves among themselves, are not wise. But we will not boast of things without our measure, but according to the measure of the rule which God hath distributed to us, a measure to reach even unto you."

No standard of religion is worth a moment's consideration which leaves prayer out of the account. No standard is worth any thought which does not make prayer the main thing in religion. So necessary is prayer, so fundamental in God's plan, so all important to everything like a religious life, that it enters into all Bible religion. Prayer itself is a standard, definite, emphatic, Scriptural. A life of prayer is the Divine rule. This is the pattern, just as our Lord, being a man of prayer, is the one pattern for us after whom to copy. Prayer fashions the pattern of a religious life. Prayer is the measure. Prayer molds the life.

The vague, indefinite, popular view of religion has no prayer in it. In its programme, prayer is entirely left out or put so low down and made so insignificant, that it hardly is worth mentioning. Man's standard of religion has no prayer about it.

It is God's standard at which we are to aim, not man's. It is not the opinions of men, not what they say, but what the Scriptures say. Loose notions of religion grow out of low notions of prayer. Prayerlessness begets loose, cloudy and indefinite views of what religion is. Aimless living and prayerlessness go hand in hand. Prayer sets something definite in the mind. Prayer seeks after something specific. The more definite our views as to the nature and need of prayer, the more definite will be our views of Christian experience and right living, and the less vague our views of religion. A low standard of religion lives hard by a low standard of praying.

Everything in a religious life depends upon being definite. The definiteness of our religious experiences and of our living will depend upon the defi-

niteness of our views of what religion is and of the
things of which it consists.

The Scriptures ever set before us the one standard of full consecration to God. This is the Divine
rule. This is the human side of this standard. The
sacrifice acceptable to God must be a complete one,
entire, a whole burnt offering. This is the measure
laid down in God's Word. Nothing less than this
can be pleasing to God. Nothing half-hearted can
please Him. " A living sacrifice," holy, and perfect
in all its parts, is the measurement of our service to
God. A full renunciation of self, a free recogni-
tion of God's right to us, and a sincere offering
of all to Him—this is the Divine requirement.
Nothing indefinite in that. Nothing is in that
which is governed by the opinions of others or
affected by how men live about us.

And while a life of prayer is embraced in such
a full consecration, at the same time prayer leads
up to the point where a complete consecration is
made to God. Consecration is but the silent expression of prayer. And the highest religious
standard is the measure of prayer and self-
dedication to God. The prayer-life and the consecrated life are partners in religion. They are so
closely allied they are never separated. The prayer
life is the direct fruit of entire consecration to God.
Prayer is the natural outflow of a really consecrated
life. The measure of consecration is the measure
of real prayer. No consecration is pleasing to God

which is not perfect in all its parts, just as no burnt offering of a Jew was ever acceptable to God unless it was a " whole burnt offering." And a consecration of this sort, after this Divine measurement, has in it as a basic principle, the business of praying. Consecration is made to God. Prayer has to do with God. Consecration is putting one's self entirely at the disposal of God. And God wants and commands all His consecrated ones to be praying ones. This is the one definite standard at which we must aim. Lower than this we cannot afford to seek.

A Scriptural standard of religion includes a clear religious experience. Religion is nothing if not experimental. Religion appeals to the inner consciousness. It is an experience if anything at all, and an experience in addition to a religious life. There is the internal part of religion as well as the external. Not only are we to " work out our salvation with fear and trembling," but " it is God that worketh in us to will and do of His good pleasure." There is a " good work in you," as well as a life outside to be lived. The new birth is a definite Christian experience, proved by infallible marks, appealing to the inner consciousness. The witness of the Spirit is not an indefinite, vague something, but is a definite, clear inward assurance given by the Holy Spirit that we are the children of God. In fact everything belonging to religious experience is clear and definite, bringing conscious joy, peace and love. And this is the Divine standard of religion, a standard attained by earnest, constant prayer, and a religious experience kept alive and enlarged by the same means of prayer.

An end to be gained, to which effort is to be directed, is important in every pursuit in order to give unity, energy and steadiness to it. In the Christian life, such an end is all important. Without a high standard before us to be gained, for which we are earnestly seeking, lassitude will unnerve effort, and past experience will taint or exhale into mere sentiment, or be hardened into cold, loveless principle.

We must go on. " Therefore, leaving the principles of the doctrine of Christ, let us go on unto perfection." The present ground we occupy must be held by making advances, and all the future must be covered and brightened by it. In religion, we must not only go on. We must know where we are going to. This is all important. It is essential that in going on in religious experience, we have something definite in view, and strike out for that one point. To ever go on and not to know to which place we are going, is altogether too vague and indefinite, and is like a man who starts out on a journey and does not have any destination in view. It is important that we lose not sight of the starting point in a religious life, and that we measure the steps already trod. But it is likewise necessary that the end be kept in view and that the steps necessary to reach the standard be always in the eye.

# X

## PRAYER BORN OF COMPASSION

"Open your New Testament, take it with you to your knees, and set Jesus Christ out of it before you. Are you like David in the sixty-third Psalm? Is your soul thirsting for God, and is your flesh longing for God in a dry and thirsty land where no water is? Then set Jesus at the well of Samaria before the eyes of your thirsty heart. And, again set Him before your heart when He stood on the last day, that great day of the feast, and cried, saying, 'If any man thirst let him come to me and drink.' Or, are you like David after the matter of Uriah? 'For, day and night, thy hand was heavy upon me: my moisture is turned into the drouth of summer.' Then set Him before you who says: 'I am not come to call the righteous, but sinners to repentance. They that be whole need not a physician, but they that are sick.' . . . Or are you the unhappy father of a prodigal son? Then, set your Father in heaven always before you: and set the Son of God always before you as He composes and preaches the parable of all parables for you and your son."

—Dr. Alexander Whyte

WE speak here more particularly of spiritual compassion, that which is born in a renewed heart, and which finds hospitality there. This compassion has in it the quality of mercy, is of the nature of pity, and moves the soul with tenderness of feeling for others. Compassion is moved at the sight of sin, sorrow and suffering. It stands at the other extreme to indifference of spirit to the wants and woes of others, and is far removed from insensibility and hardness of heart, in the midst of want and trouble and wretchedness. Compassion stands besides sympathy for others, is interested in them, and is concerned about them.

That which excites and develops compassion and puts it to work, is the sight of multitudes in want and distress, and helpless to relieve themselves. Helplessness especially appeals to compassion. Compassion is silent but does not remain secluded. It goes out at the sight of trouble, sin and need. Compassion runs out in earnest prayer, first of all, for those for whom it feels, and has a sympathy for them. Prayer for others is born of a sympathetic heart. Prayer is natural and almost spontaneous when compassion is begotten in the heart. Prayer belongs to the compassionate man.

There is a certain compassion which belongs to the natural man, which expends its force in simple gifts to those in need, not to be despised. But spiritual compassion, the kind born in a renewed heart, which is Christly in its nature, is deeper, broader and more prayerlike. Christly compassion always moves to prayer. This sort of compassion goes beyond the relief of mere bodily wants, and saying, " Be ye warmed—be ye clothed." It reaches deeper down and goes much farther.

Compassion is not blind. Rather we should say, that compassion is not born of blindness. He who has compassion of soul has eyes, first of all, to see the things which excite compassion. He who has no eyes to see the exceeding sinfulness of sin, the wants and woes of humanity, will never have compassion for humanity. It is written of our Lord that "when he saw the multitudes, he was moved with compassion on them." First, seeing the multitudes, with their hunger, their woes and their helpless condition, then compassion. Then prayer for the multitudes. Hard is he, and far from being Christlike, who sees the multitudes, and is unmoved at the sight of their sad state, their unhappiness and their peril. He has no heart of prayer for men.

Compassion may not always move men, but is always moved *toward* men. Compassion may not always turn men to God, but it will, and does, turn God to man. And where it is most helpless to relieve the needs of others, it can at least break out into prayer to God for others. Compassion is never indifferent, selfish, and forgetful of others. Compassion has alone to do with others. The fact that the multitudes were as sheep having no shepherd, was the one thing which appealed to our Lord's compassionate nature. Then their hunger moved Him, and the sight of the sufferings and diseases of these multitudes stirred the pity of His heart.

> "Father of mercies, send Thy grace
> All powerful from above,
> To form in our obedient souls
> The image of Thy love.

"O may our sympathising breasts
    That generous pleasure know;
Kindly to share in others' joy,
    And weep for others' woe."

But compassion has not alone to do with the body
and its disabilities and needs. The soul's distressing state, its needs and danger all appeal to compassion. The highest state of grace is known by the
infallible mark of compassion for poor sinners.
This sort of compassion belongs to grace, and sees
not alone the bodies of men, but their immortal
spirits, soiled by sin, unhappy in their condition
without God, and in imminent peril of being forever lost. When compassion beholds this sight of
dying men hurrying to the bar of God, then it is
that it breaks out into intercessions for sinful men.
Then it is that compassion speaks out after this
fashion:

"But feeble my compassion proves,
    And can but weep where most it loves;
Thy own all saving arm employ,
    And turn these drops of grief to joy."

The Prophet Jeremiah declares this about God,
giving the reason why sinners are not consumed
by His wrath:

"It is of the Lord's mercies we are not consumed,
because his compassions fail not."

And it is this Divine quality in us which makes us so much like God. So we find the Psalmist describing the righteous man who is pronounced blessed by God: " He is gracious and full of compassion, and righteous."

And as giving great encouragement to penitent praying sinners, the Psalmist thus records some of the striking attributes of the Divine character: " The Lord is gracious and full of compassion, slow to anger, and of great mercy."

It is no wonder, then, that we find it recorded several times of our Lord while on earth that " he was moved with compassion." Can any one doubt that His compassion moved Him to pray for those suffering, sorrowing ones who came across His pathway?

Paul was wonderfully interested in the religious welfare of his Jewish brethren, was concerned over them, and his heart was strangely warmed with tender compassion for their salvation, even though mistreated and sorely persecuted by them. In writing to the Romans, we hear him thus express himself:

" I say the truth in Christ, I lie not, my conscience also bearing me witness in the Holy Ghost, that I have great heaviness and continual sorrow in my heart; for I could wish that myself were accursed for my brethren, my kinsmen according to the flesh."

What marvellous compassion is here described

for Paul's own nation! What wonder that a little later on he records his desire and prayer:

" Brethren, my heart's desire and prayer to God for Israel is that they might be saved."

We have an interesting case in Matthew which gives us an account of what excited so largely the compassion of our Lord at one time:

" But when he saw the multitudes, he was moved with compassion on them, because they fainted, and were scattered abroad, as sheep having no shepherd. Then saith he unto his disciples, The harvest truly is plenteous, but the labourers are few. Pray ye therefore the Lord of the harvest, that he will send forth labourers into his harvest."

It seems from parallel statements that our Lord had called His disciples aside to rest awhile, exhausted as He and they were by the excessive drafts on them, by the ceaseless contact with the persons who were ever coming and going, and by their exhaustive toil in ministering to the immense multitudes. But the multitudes precede Him, and instead of finding wilderness-solitude, quiet and repose, He finds great multitudes eager to see and hear, and to be healed. His compassions are moved. The ripened harvests need labourers. He did not call these labourers at once, by sovereign authority, but charges the disciples to betake themselves to God in prayer, asking Him to send forth labourers into His harvest.

Here is the urgency of prayer enforced by the compassions of our Lord. It is prayer born of compassion for perishing humanity. Prayer is pressed on the Church for labourers to be sent into the harvest of the Lord. The harvest will go to waste and perish without the labourers, while the labourers must be God-chosen, God-sent, and God-commissioned. But God does not send these labourers into His harvest without prayer. The failure of the labourers is owing to the failure of prayer. The scarcity of labourers in the harvest is due to the fact that the Church fails to pray for labourers according to His command.

The ingathering of the harvests of earth for the granaries of heaven is dependent on the prayers of God's people. Prayer secures the labourers sufficient in quantity and in quality for all the needs of the harvest. God's chosen labourers, God's endowed labourers, and God's thrust-forth labourers, are the only ones who will truly go, filled with Christly compassion and endued with Christly power, whose going will avail, and these are secured by prayer. Christ's people on their knees with Christ's compassion in their hearts for dying men and for needy souls, exposed to eternal peril, is the pledge of labourers in numbers and character to meet the wants of earth and the purposes of heaven.

God is sovereign of the earth and of heaven, and the choice of labourers in His harvest He delegates to no one else. Prayer honours Him as sovereign and moves Him to His wise and holy selection. We will have to put prayer to the front ere the fields of paganism will be successfully tilled for Christ. God knows His men, and He likewise knows full well His work. Prayer gets God to send forth the best men and the most fit men and the men best qualified to work in the harvest. Moving the missionary cause by forces this side of God has been its bane, its weakness and its failure. Compassion for the world of sinners, fallen in Adam, but redeemed in Christ will move the Church to pray for them and stir the Church to pray the Lord of the harvest to send forth labourers into the harvest.

> " Lord of the harvest hear
>   Thy needy servants' cry;
> Answer our faith's effectual prayer,
>   And all our wants supply.

> " Convert and send forth more
>   Into Thy Church abroad;
> And let them speak Thy word of power,
>   As workers with their God."

What a comfort and what hope there is to fill our breasts when we think of one in Heaven who ever liveth to intercede for us, because " His compassion fails not!" Above everything else, we have a compassionate Saviour, one "who can have compassion on the ignorant, and on them who are out of the way, for that he himself is compassed about with infirmity." The compassion of our Lord well fits Him for being the Great High Priest of Adam's fallen, lost and helpless race.

And if He is filled with such compassion that it moves Him at the Father's right hand to intercede for us, then by every token we should have the same compassion on the ignorant and those out of the way, exposed to Divine wrath, as would move us to pray for them. Just in so far as we are compassionate will we be prayerful for others. Compassion does not expend its force in simply saying, "Be ye warmed; be ye clothed," but drives us to our knees in prayer for those who need Christ and His grace.

> "The Son of God in tears
>     The wondering angels see;
> Be thou astonished, O my soul!
>     He shed those tears for thee.
>
> "He wept that we might weep;
>     Each sin demands a tear;
> In heaven alone no sin is found,
>     And there's no weeping there."

Jesus Christ was altogether man. While He was the Divine Son of God yet at the same time, He was the human Son of God. Christ had a pre-eminently human side, and, here, compassion reigned. He was tempted in all points as we are, yet without sin. At one time how the flesh seems to have weakened under the fearful strain upon Him, and how He must have inwardly shrunk under the pain and pull! Looking up to heaven, He prays, " Father, save me from this hour." How the spirit nerves and holds —" but for this cause came I to this hour." Only he can solve this mystery who has followed His Lord in straits and gloom and pain, and realised that the " spirit is willing but the flesh is weak."

All this but fitted our Lord to be a compassionate Saviour. It is no sin to feel the pain and realise the darkness on the path into which God leads. It is only human to cry out against the pain, the terror, and desolation of that hour. It is Divine to cry out to God in that hour, even while shrinking and sinking down, " For this cause came I unto this hour." Shall I fail through the weakness of the flesh? No. " Father, glorify thy name." How strong it makes us, and how true, to have one pole star to guide us to the glory of God!

# XI

## CONCERTED PRAYER

"A tourist, in climbing an Alpine summit, finds himself tied by a strong rope to his trusty guide, and to three of his fellow-tourists. As they skirt a perilous precipice he cannot pray, 'Lord, hold up *my* goings in a safe path, that *my* footsteps slip not, but as to my guide and companions, they must look out for themselves.' The only proper prayer in such a case is, 'Lord, hold up *our* goings in a safe path; for if one slips all of us may perish.'"—H. CLAY TRUMBULL

THE pious Quesnel says that "God is found in union and agreement. Nothing is more efficacious than this in prayer."

Intercessions combine with prayers and supplications. The word does not mean necessarily prayer in relation to others. It means a coming together, a falling in with a most intimate friend for free, unrestrained communion. It implies prayer, free, familiar and bold.

Our Lord deals with this question of the concert of prayer in the eighteenth chapter of Matthew. He deals with the benefit and energy resulting from the aggregation of prayer forces. The prayer principle and the prayer promise will be best understood in the connection in which it was made by our Lord:

" Moreover, if thy brother shall trespass against thee, go and tell him his fault between thee and him alone: if he shall hear thee, thou hast gained thy brother. But if he will not hear thee, then take with thee one or two more, that in the mouth of two or three witnesses, every word may be established.

" And if he shall neglect to hear them, tell it unto the church; but if he neglect to hear the church, let him be unto thee as an heathen and a publican.

" Verily I say unto you, Whatsoever ye shall bind on earth, shall be bound in heaven; and whatsoever ye shall loose on earth, shall be loosed in heaven. Again I say unto you, That if two of you shall agree on earth as touching any thing that they shall ask, it shall be done for them of my Father which is in heaven. For where two or three are gathered together in my name, there am I in the midst of them."

This represents the Church in prayer to enforce discipline in order that its members who have been overtaken by faults, may yield readily to the disciplinary process. In addition, it is the Church called together in a concert of prayer in order to repair the waste and friction ensuing upon the cutting off of a Church offender. This last direction as to a concert of prayer is that the whole matter may be referred to Almighty God for His approval and ratification.

All this means that the main, the concluding and the all powerful agency in the Church is prayer, whether it be, as we have seen in Matthew, 9th chapter, to thrust out labourers into God's earthly harvest fields, or to exclude from the Church a violator of unity, law and order, who will neither listen to his brethren nor repent and confess his fault.

It means that Church discipline, now a lost art in the modern Church, must go hand in hand with prayer, and that the Church which has no disposition to separate wrong doers from the Church, and which has no excommunication spirit for incorrigible offenders against law and order, will have no communication with God. Church purity must precede the Church's prayers. The unity of discipline in the Church precedes the unity of prayers by the Church.

Let it be noted with emphasis that a Church which is careless of discipline will be careless in praying. A Church which tolerates evil doers in its communion, will cease to pray, will cease to pray with agreement, and will cease to be a Church gathered together in prayer in Christ's name.

This matter of Church discipline is an important one in the Scriptures. The need of watchfulness over the lives of its members belongs to the Church of God. The Church is an organization for mutual help, and it is charged with the watch care of all of its members. Disorderly conduct cannot be passed by unnnoticed. The course of procedure in such cases is clearly given in the eighteenth chapter of Matthew, which has been heretofore referred to. Furthermore, Paul, in Galatians 6: 1, gives explicit directions as to those who fall into sin in the Church:

"Brethren, if a man be overtaken in a fault, ye which are spiritual restore such a one in the spirit of meekness, considering thyself lest thou also be tempted."

The work of the Church is not alone to seek members but it is to watch over and guard them after they have entered the Church. And if any are overtaken by sin, they must be sought out, and if they cannot be cured of their faults, then excision must take place. This is the doctrine our Lord lays down.

It is somewhat striking that the Church at Ephesus, (Rev. 2) though it had left its first love, and had sadly declined in vital godliness and in those things which make up spiritual life, yet it receives credit for this good quality: "Thou canst not bear them that are evil."

While the Church at Pergamos was admonished because it had there among its membership those who taught such hurtful doctrines that were a stumbling-block to others. And not so much that such characters were in the Church, but that they were tolerated. The impression is that the Church leaders were blind to the presence of such hurtful characters, and hence were indisposed to administer discipline. This indisposition was an unfailing sign of prayerlessness in the membership. There was no union of prayer effort looking to cleansing the Church and keeping it clean.

This disciplinary idea stands out prominently in

the Apostle Paul's writings to the Churches. The Church at Corinth had a notorious case of fornication where a man had married his step-mother, and this Church had been careless about this iniquity. Paul rather sharply reproved this Church and gave explicit command to this effect: "Therefore put away from among yourselves that wicked person." Here was concert of action on the part of praying people demanded by Paul.

As good a Church as that at Thessalonica needed instruction and caution on this matter of looking after disorderly persons. So we hear Paul saying unto them:

"Now we command you, brethren, in the name of our Lord Jesus Christ, that ye withdraw yourselves from every brother that walketh disorderly."

Mark you. It is not the mere presence of disorderly persons in a Church which merits the displeasure of God. It is when they are tolerated under the mistaken plea of "bearing with them," and no steps are taken either to cure them of their evil practices or exclude them from the fellowship of the Church. And this glaring neglect on the part of the Church of its wayward members, is but a sad sign of a lack of praying, for a praying Church, given to mutual praying, agreement praying, is keen to discern when a brother is overtaken in a fault, and seeks either to restore him, or to cut him off if he be incorrigible.

Much of this dates back to the lack of spiritual vision on the part of Church leaders. The Lord by the mouth of the Prophet Isaiah once asked the very pertinent, suggestive question, " And who is blind but my servant? " This blindness in leadership in the Church is no more patent than in this question of seeing evil doers in the Church, in caring for them, and when the effort to restore them fails, to withdraw fellowship from them, and let them be " as a heathen man and a publican." The truth is there is such a lust for members in the Church in these modern times, that the officials and preachers have entirely lost sight of the members who have violated baptismal covenants, and who are living in open disregard of God's Word. The idea now is *quantity* in membership, *not quality*. The purity of the Church is put in the background in the craze to secure numbers, and to pad the Church rolls and make large figures in statistical columns. Prayer, much prayer, mutual prayer, would bring the Church back to Scriptural standards, and would purge the Church of many wrongdoers, while it might cure not a few of their evil lives.

Prayer and Church discipline are not new revelations of the Christian dispensation. These two things had a high place in the Jewish Church. Instances are too numerous to mention all of them. Ezra is a case in point. When he returned from the captivity, he found a sad and distressing condition of things among the Lord's people who were left in the land. They had not separated themselves from the surrounding heathen people, and had intermarried with them, contrary to Divine commands. And those high in the Church were involved, the priests and the Levites with others. Ezra was greatly moved at the account given him, and rent his garments and wept and prayed. Evil doers in the Church did not meet his approval, nor did he shut his eyes to them nor excuse them, neither did he compromise the situation. When he had finished confessing the sins of the people and his praying, the people assembled themselves before him and joined him in a covenant agreement to put away from them their evil doings, and wept and prayed in company with Ezra.

The result was that the people thoroughly repented of their transgressions, and Israel was reformed. Praying and a good man, who was neither blind nor unconcerned, did the deed.

Of Ezra it is written, "For he mourned because of the transgression of them that had been carried away." So it is with every praying man in the Church when he has eyes to see the transgression of evil doers in the Church, who has a heart to grieve over them, and who has a spirit in him so concerned about the Church that he prays about it.

Blessed is that Church who has praying leaders, who can see that which is disorderly in the Church, who are grieved about it, and who put forth their hands to correct the evils which harm God's cause

as a weight to its progress. One point in the indict-
ment against those " Who are at ease in Zion," referred to by Amos, is that " they are not grieved for
the affliction of Joseph." And this same indict-
ment could be brought against Church leaders of
modern times. They are not grieved because the
members are engulfed in a craze for worldly, carnal
things, nor when there are those in the Church
walking openly in disorder, whose lives scandalise
religion. Of course such leaders do not pray over
the matter, for praying would beget a spirit of
solicitude in them for these evil doers, and would
drive away the spirit of unconcern which possesses them.

It would be well for prayerless Church leaders
and careless pastors to read the account of the ink
horn man in Ezekiel, 9th chapter, where God in-
structed the prophet to send through the city certain men who would destroy those in the city
because of the great evils found therein. But certain persons were to be spared. These were they
who " sigh and cry for all the abominations that be
done in the midst of the city." The man with the
ink horn was to mark every one of these sighers
and mourners so that they would escape the im-
pending destruction. Please note that the instruc-
tions were that the slaying of those who did not
mourn and sigh should " Begin at my sanctuary."

What a lesson for non-praying, unconcerned officials of the modern Church! How few there are

who " sigh and cry " for present-day abominations
in the land, and who are grieved over the desola-
tions of Zion! What need for "two or three to
be gathered together " in a concert of prayer over
these conditions, and in the secret place weep and
pray for the sins in Zion!

This concert òf prayer, this agreement in praying, taught by our Lord in the eighteenth chapter
of Matthew, finds proof and illustration elsewhere.
This was the kind of prayer which Paul referred to
in his request to his Roman brethren, recorded in
Romans 15 : 30:

" Now I beseech you, brethren, for the Lord Jesus
Christ's sake, and for the love of the Spirit, that ye
strive together with me in your prayers to God for
me; that I may be delivered from them that do not
believe in Judea.'

Here is unity in prayer, prayer by agreement, and
prayer which drives directly at deliverance from
unbelieving and evil men, the same kind of prayer
urged by our Lord, and the end practically the
same, deliverance from unbelieving men, that deliverance wrought either by bringing them to repentance or by exclusion from the Church.

The same idea is found in II Thessalonians 3 : 1:

" Finally, brethren, pray for us that the word of the
Lord may have free course and be glorified, even as it
is with you; and that we may be delivered from unreasonable and wicked men."

Here is united prayer requested by an Apostle, among other things, for deliverance from wicked men, that same that the Church of God needs in this day. By joining their prayers to his, there was the desired end of riddance from men who were hurtful to the Church of God and who were a hindrance to the running of the Word of the Lord. Let us ask, are there not in the present-day Church those who are a positive hindrance to the on-going of the Word of the Lord? What better course is there than to jointly pray over the question, at the same time using the Christ-given course of discipline first to save them, but failing in that course, to excise them from the body?

Does that seem a harsh course? Then our Lord was guilty of harshness Himself, for He ends these directions by saying, " But if he neglect to hear the Church, let him be unto thee as a heathen man and a publican."

No more is this harshness than is the act of the skilful surgeon, who sees the whole body and its members endangered by a gangrenous limb, and severs the limb from the body for the good of the whole. No more was it harshness in the captain and crew of the vessel on which Jonah was found, when the storm arose threatening destruction to all on board, to cast the fleeing prophet overboard. What seems harshness is obedience to God, is for the welfare of the Church, and is wise in the extreme.

# XII

## THE UNIVERSALITY OF PRAYER

"It takes more of the power of the Spirit to make the farm, the home, the office, the store, the shop holy than it does to make the Church holy. It takes more of the power of the Spirit to make Saturday holy than to make Sunday holy. It takes much more of the power of the Spirit to make money for God than it does to make a talk for God. Much more to live a great life for God than to preach a great sermon."—EDWARD M. BOUNDS

PRAYER is far-reaching in its influence and world-wide in its effects. It affects all men, affects them everywhere, and affects them in all things. It touches man's interest in time and eternity. It lays hold upon God and moves Him to interfere in the affairs of earth. It moves the angels to minister to men in this life. It restrains and defeats the devil in his schemes to ruin man. Prayer goes everywhere and lays its hand upon everything. There is a universality in prayer. When we talk about prayer and its work we must use universal terms. It is individual in its application and benefits, but it is general and world-wide at the same time in its good influences. It blesses man in every event of life, furnishes him help in every emergency, and gives him comfort in every trouble. There is no experience through which man is called to go but prayer is there as a helper, a comforter and a guide.

When we speak of the universality of prayer, we discover many sides to it. First, it may be remarked that all men ought to pray. Prayer is intended for all men, because all men need God and need what God has and what prayer only can secure. As men are called upon to pray everywhere, by consequence all men must pray for men are everywhere. Universal terms are used when men are commanded to pray, while there is a promise in universal terms to all who call upon God for pardon, for mercy and for help:

" For there is no difference; for the same Lord over all is rich unto all that call upon him. For whosoever shall call upon the name of the Lord shall be saved."

As there is no difference in the state of sin in which men are found, and all men need the saving grace of God which only can bless them, and as this saving grace is obtained only in answer to prayer, therefore all men are called on to pray because of their very needs.

It is a rule of Scriptural interpretation that whenever a command issues with no limitation, it is universal in binding force. So the words of the Lord in Isaiah are to the point:

" Seek ye the Lord while he may be found; call ye upon him while he is near. Let the wicked forsake his way, and the unrighteous man his thoughts, and let him return unto the Lord, who will have mercy, and to our God who will abundantly pardon."

So that as wickedness is universal, and as pardon is needed by all men, so all men must seek the Lord while he may be found, and must call upon Him while he is near. Prayer belongs to all men because all men are redeemed in Christ. It is a privilege for every man to pray, but it is no less a bounden duty for them to call upon God. No sinner is debarred from the mercy seat. All are welcomed to approach the throne of grace with all their wants and woes, with all their sins and burdens.

> " Come all the world, come, sinner thou,
> All things in Christ are ready now."

Whenever a poor sinner turns his eyes to God, no matter where he is nor what his guilt and sinfulness, the eye of God is upon him and His ear is opened to his prayers.

But men may pray everywhere, since God is accessible in every clime and under all circumstances. " I will therefore that men pray everywhere, lifting up holy hands, without wrath and doubting."

No locality is too distant from God on earth to reach heaven. No place is so remote that God cannot see and hear one who looks toward Him and seeks His face. Oliver Holden puts into a hymn these words:

" Then, my soul, in every strait,
  To Thy Father come and wait;
  He will answer every prayer;
  God is present everywhere."

There is just this modification of the idea that
one can pray everywhere.  Some places, because of
the evil business carried on there, or because of the
environments which belong there, growing out of
the place itself, the moral character of those who
carry on the business, and of those who support it,
are localities where prayer would not be in place.
We might instance the saloon, the theatre, the
opera, the card table, the dance, and other like
places of worldly amusement.  Prayer is so much
out of place at such places that no one would ever
presume to pray.  Prayer would be an intrusion, so
regarded by the owners, the patrons and the sup-
porters of such places.  Furthermore those who attend such places are not praying people.  They
belong almost entirely to the prayerless crowd of
worldlings.

While we are to pray everywhere, it unques-
tionably means that we are not to frequent places
where we cannot pray.  To pray everywhere is to
pray in all legitimate places, and to attend especially
those places where prayer is welcome, and is given a
gracious hospitality.  To pray everywhere is to pre-
serve the spirit of prayer in places of business, in
our intercourse with men, and in the privacy of the
home amid all of its domestic cares.

The Model Prayer of our Lord, called familiarly
" The Lord's Prayer," is the universal prayer, because it is peculiarly adapted to all men everywhere
in all circumstances in all times of need.  It can be
put in the mouths of all people in all nations, and in
all times.  It is a model of praying which needs no
amendment nor alteration for every family, people
and nation.

Furthermore, prayer has its universal application in that all men are to be the subjects of
prayer.  All men everywhere are to be prayed
for.  Prayer must take in all of Adam's fallen
race because all men are fallen in Adam, redeemed
in Christ, and are benefited by prayers for them.
This is Paul's doctrine in his prayer directory in
I Timothy 2:1:

" I exhort, therefore, that first of all, supplications,
prayers, intercessions and giving of thanks be made
for all men."

There is strong Scriptural warrant, therefore, for
reaching out and embracing all men in our prayers,
since not only are we commanded thus to pray for
them, but the reason given is that Christ gave Himself a ransom for all men, and all men are provision-
ally beneficiaries of the atoning death of Jesus
Christ.

But lastly, and more at length, prayer has a universal side in that all things which concern us are to
be prayed about, while all things which are for our

good, physical, social, intellectual, spiritual, and eternal, are subjects of prayer. Before, however, we consider this phase of prayer let us stop and again look at the universal prayer for all men. As a special class to be prayed for, we may mention those who have control in state or who bear rule in the Church. Prayer has mighty potencies. It makes good rulers, and makes them better rulers. It restrains the lawless and the despotic. Rulers are to be prayed for. They are not out of the reach and the control of prayer, because they are not out of the reach and control of God. Wicked Nero was on the throne of Rome when Paul wrote these words to Timothy urging prayer for those in authority.

Christian lips are to breathe prayers for the cruel and infamous rulers in state as well as for the righteous and the benign governors and princes. Prayer is to be as far-reaching as the race, " for all men." Humanity is to burden our hearts as we pray, and all men are to engage our thoughts in approaching a throne of grace. In our praying hours, all men must have a place. The wants and woes of the entire race are to broaden and make tender our sympathies, and inflame our petitions. No little man can pray. No man with narrow views of God, of His plan to save men, and of the universal needs of all men, can pray effectually. It takes a broad-minded man, who understands God and His purposes in the atonement, to pray well. No cynic can pray.    Prayer is the divinest philanthropy, as well as giant-great-heartedness.    Prayer comes from a big heart, filled with thoughts about all men and with sympathies for all men.

Prayer runs parallel with the will of God, " who will have all men to be saved and to come unto the knowledge of the truth."

Prayer reaches up to heaven, and brings heaven down to earth.    Prayer has in its hands a double blessing.    It rewards him who prays, and blesses him who is prayed for.    It brings peace to warring passions and calms warring elements.    Tranquillity is the happy fruit of true praying.    There is an inner calm which comes to him who prays and an outer calm as well.    Prayer creates " quiet and peaceable lives in all godliness and honesty."

Right praying not only makes life beautiful in peace, but redolent in righteousness and weighty in influence.    Honesty, gravity, integrity and weight in character are the natural and essential fruits of prayer.

It is this kind of world-wide, large-hearted, un-selfish praying which pleases God well, and which is acceptable in His sight, because it co-operates with His will and runs in gracious streams to all men and to each man.    It is this kind of praying which the man Christ Jesus did when on earth, and the same kind which He is now doing at His Father's right hand in heaven, as our Mighty Intercessor.    He is the pattern of prayer.    He is between God and man, the one Mediator, who gave Himself a ransom for all men, and for each man.

So it is that true prayer links itself to the will of God, and runs in streams of solicitude, and compassion, and intercession for all men. As Jesus Christ died for every one involved in the fall, so prayer girdles every one and gives itself for the benefit of every one. Like our one Mediator between God and man, he who prays stands midway between God and man, with prayers, supplications, " and strong cryings and tears." Prayer holds in its grasp the movements of the race of man, and embraces the destinies of men for all eternity. The king and the beggar are both affected by it. It touches heaven and moves earth. Prayer holds earth to heaven and brings heaven in close contact with earth.

> " Your guides and brethren bear
>     Forever on your mind;
> Extend the arms of mighty prayer
>     In grasping all mankind."

# XIII

## PRAYER AND MISSIONS

"One day, about this time, I heard an unusual bleating amongst my few remaining goats, as if they were being killed or tortured. I rushed to the goat-house and found myself instantly surrounded by a band of armed men. The snare had caught me, their weapons were raised, and I expected the next moment to die. But God moved me to talk to them firmly and kindly; I warned them of their sin and its punishment; I showed them that only my love and pity led me to remain there seeking their good, and that if they killed me they killed their best friend. I further assured them I was not afraid to die, for at death my Saviour would take me to heaven and that I would be far happier than on earth; and that my only desire to live was to make them happy by teaching them to love Jesus Christ my Lord. I then lifted up my hands and eyes to the heavens and prayed aloud for Jesus to bless all my Tannese and to protect me or take me to heaven as He saw to be for the best. One after another they slipped away from me and Jesus restrained them again. Did ever mother run more quickly to protect her crying child in danger's hour than the Lord Jesus hastens to answer believing prayer and send help to His servants in His own good time and way, so far as it shall be for their good and His glory."—John G. Paton

MISSIONS mean the giving of the Gospel to those of Adam's fallen race who have never heard of Christ and His atoning death. It means the giving to others the opportunity to hear of salvation through our Lord Jesus Christ, and allowing others to have a chance to receive, and accept the blessings of the Gospel, as we have it in Christianised lands. It means that those who enjoy the benefits of the Gospel give these same religious advantages and Gospel privileges to all of mankind. Prayer has a great deal to do with missions. Prayer is the hand-maid of missions. The success of all real missionary effort is dependent on prayer. The life and spirit of missions are the life and spirit of prayer. Both prayer and missions were born in the Divine Mind. Prayer and missions are bosom companions. Prayer creates and makes missions successful, while missions lean heavily on prayer. In the seventy-second Psalm, one which deals with the Messiah, it is stated that "prayer shall be made for him continually." Prayer would be made for His coming to save man, and prayer would be made for the success of the plan of salvation which He would come to set on foot.

The Spirit of Jesus Christ is the spirit of missions. Our Lord Jesus Christ was Himself the first missionary. His promise and advent composed the first missionary movement. The missionary spirit is not simply a phase of the Gospel, not a mere feature of the plan of salvation, but is its very spirit and life. The missionary movement is the Church of Jesus Christ marching in militant array, with the design of possessing the whole world of mankind for Christ. Whoever is touched by the Spirit of God is fired by the missionary spirit. An anti-missionary Christian is a contradiction in terms. We might say that it would be impossible to be an anti-missionary Christian because of the impossibility for the Divine and human forces to put men in such a state as not to align them with the missionary cause. Missionary impulse is the heart-beat of our Lord Jesus Christ, sending the vital forces of Himself through the whole body of the Church. The spiritual life of God's people rises or falls with the force of those heart-beats. When these life forces cease, then death ensues. So that anti-missionary Churches are dead Churches, just as anti-missionary Christians are dead Christians.

The craftiest wile of Satan, if he cannot prevent a great movement for God, is to debauch the movement. If he can put the movement first, and the spirit of the movement in the background, he has materialised and thoroughly debauched the movement. Mighty prayer only will save the movement from being materialised, and keep the spirit of the movement strong and controlling.

The key of all missionary success is prayer. That key is in the hands of the home churches. The trophies won by our Lord in heathen lands will be won by praying missionaries, not by professional workers in foreign lands. More especially will this success be won by saintly praying in the churches at home. The home church on her knees fasting and praying, is the great base of spiritual supplies, the sinews of war, and the pledge of victory in this dire and final conflict. Financial resources are not the real sinews of war in this fight. Machinery in itself carries no power to break down heathen walls, open effectual doors and win heathen hearts to Christ. Prayer alone can do the deed.

Aaron and Hur did not more surely give victory to Israel through Moses, than a praying church through Jesus Christ will give victory on every battlefield in heathen lands. It is as true in foreign fields as it is in home lands. The praying church wins the contest. The home church has done but a paltry thing when she has furnished the money to establish missions and support her missionaries. Money is important, but money without prayer is powerless in the face of the darkness, the wretchedness and the sin in unchristianised lands. Prayerless giving breeds barrenness and death. Poor praying at home is the solution of poor results in the foreign field. Prayerless giving is the secret of all crises in the missionary movements of the day, and is the occasion of the accumulation of debts in missionary boards.

It is all right to urge men to give of their means to the missionary cause. But it is much more important to urge them to give their prayers to the movement. Foreign missions need, today, more the power of prayer than the power of money. Prayer can make even poverty in the missionary cause move on amidst difficulties and hindrances. Much money without prayer is helpless and powerless in the face of the utter darkness and sin and wretchedness on the foreign field.

This is peculiarly a missionary age. Protestant Christianity is stirred as it never was before in the line of aggression in pagan lands. The missionary movement has taken on proportions that awaken hope, kindle enthusiasm, and which demand the attention, if not the interest, of the coldest and the most lifeless. Nearly every Church has caught the contagion, and the sails of their proposed missionary movements are spread wide to catch the favouring breezes. Herein is the danger just now, that the missionary movement will go ahead of the missionary spirit. This has always been the peril of the Church, losing the substance in the shade, losing the spirit in the outward shell, and contenting itself in the mere parade of the movement, putting the force of effort in the movement and not in the spirit.

The magnificence of this movement may not only blind us to the spirit of it, but the spirit which should give life and shape to the movement may be lost in the wealth of the movement as the ship, borne by favouring winds, may be lost when these winds swell to a storm.

Not a few of us have heard eloquent and earnest speeches stressing the imperative need of money for missions where we have heard one stressing the imperative need of prayer. All our plans and devices drive to the one end of raising money, not to quicken faith and promote prayer. The common idea among Church leaders is that if we get the money, prayer will come as a matter of course. The very reverse is the truth. If we get the Church at the business of praying, and thus secure the spirit of missions, money will more than likely come as a matter of course. Spiritual agencies and spiritual forces never come as a matter of course. Spiritual duties and spiritual factors, left to the " matter of course " law, will surely fall out and die. Only the things which are stressed live and rule in the spiritual realm. They who give, will not necessarily pray. Many in our churches are liberal givers who are noted for their prayerlessness. One of the evils of the present-day missionary movement lies just there. Giving is entirely removed from prayer. Prayer receives scant attention, while giving stands out prominently. They who truly pray will be moved to give. Praying creates the giving spirit. The praying ones will give liberally and self-denyingly. He who enters his closet to God, will also open his purse to God. But perfunctory, grudging, assessment-giving kills the very spirit of prayer. Emphasising the material to the neglect of the spiritual, by an inexorable law retires and discounts the spiritual.

It is truly wonderful how great a part money plays in the modern religious movements, and how little prayer plays in them. In striking contrast with that statement, it is marvellous how little part money played in primitive Christianity as a factor in spreading the Gospel, and how wonderful part prayer played in it.

The grace of giving is nowhere cultured to a richer growth than in the closet. If all our missionary boards and secretaryships were turned into praying bands, until the agony of real prayer and travail with Christ for a perishing world came on them, real estate, bank stocks, United States bonds would be in the market for the spreading of Christ's Gospel among men. If the spirit of prayer prevailed, missionary boards whose individual members are worth millions, would not be staggering under a load of debt and great Churches would not have a yearly deficit and a yearly grumbling, grudging, and pressure to pay a beggarly assessment to support a mere handful of missionaries, with the additional humiliation of debating the question of recalling some of them. The on-going of Christ's kingdom is locked up in the closet of prayer by Christ Himself, and not in the contribution box.

The Prophet Isaiah, looking down the centuries with the vision of a seer, thus expresses his purpose to continue in prayer and give God no rest till Christ's kingdom be established among men:

" For Zion's sake will I not hold my peace, and for Jerusalem's sake I will not rest till the righteousness thereof goeth forth as brightness, and the salvation thereof as a lamp that burneth."

Then, foretelling the final success of the Christian Church, he thus speaks:

" And the Gentiles shall see thy righteousness, and all kings thy glory, and thou shalt be called by a new name, which the mouth of the Lord shall name."

Then the Lord, Himself, by the mouth of this Evangelical prophet, declares as follows:

" I have set watchmen upon thy walls, O Jerusalem, which shall never hold their peace, day nor night. Ye that make mention of the Lord, keep not silence. And give him no rest till he establish and till he make Jerusalem a praise in the earth."

In the margin of our Bible, it reads, " Ye that are the Lord's remembrancers." The idea is, that these praying ones are those who are the Lord's re- membrancers, those who remind Him of what He has promised, and who give Him no rest till God's Church is established in the earth.

And one of the leading petitions in the Lord's Prayer deals with this same question of the estab- lishing of God's kingdom and the progress of the Gospel in the short, pointed petition, " Thy king- dom come," with the added words, " Thy will be done on earth as it is done in heaven."

The missionary movement in the Apostolic Church was born in an atmosphere of fasting and prayer. The very movement looking to offering the blessings of the Christian Church to the Gentiles was on the housetop on the occasion when Peter went up there to pray, and God showed him His Divine purpose to extend the privileges of the Gospel to the Gentiles, and to break down the middle wall of partition between Jew and Gentile.

But more specifically Paul and Barnabas were definitely called and set apart to the missionary field at Antioch when the Church there had fasted and prayed. It was then the Holy Spirit answered from heaven: " Separate me Barnabas and Saul for the work whereunto I have called them."

Please note this was not the call to the ministry of Paul and Barnabas, but more particularly their definite call to the foreign field. Paul had been called to the ministry years before this, even at his conversion. This was a subsequent call to a work born of special and continued prayer in the Church at Antioch. God calls men not only to the ministry but to be missionaries. Missionary work is God's work. And it is the God-called men who are to do it. These are the kind of missionaries which have wrought well and successfully in the foreign field in the past, and the same kind will do the work in the future, or it will not be done.

It is praying missionaries who are needed for the work, and it is a praying church who sends them out, which are prophecies of the success which is promised. The sort of religion to be exported by missionaries is of the praying sort. The religion to which the heathen world is to be converted is a religion of prayer, and a religion of prayer to the true God. The heathen world already prays to its idols and false gods. But they are to be taught by praying missionaries, sent out by a praying Church, to cast away their idols and to begin to call upon the name of the Lord Jesus Christ. No prayerless church can transport to heathen lands a praying religion. No prayerless missionary can bring heathen idolaters who know not our God to their knees in true prayer until he becomes pre-eminently a man of prayer. As it takes praying men at home to do God's work, none the less does it take praying missionaries to bring those who sit in darkness to the light.

The most noted and most successful missionaries have been pre-eminently men of prayer. David Livingstone, William Taylor, Adoniram Judson, Henry Martyn, and Hudson Taylor, with many more, form a band of illustrious praying men whose impress and influence still abide where they laboured. No prayerless man is wanted for this job. Above everything else, the primary qualification for every missionary is prayer. Let him be, above everything else, a man of prayer. And when the crowning day comes, and the records are made up and read at the great judgment day, then it will appear how well praying men wrought in the hard fields of heathendom, and how much was due to them in laying the foundations of Christianity in those fields.

The one only condition which is to give world-wide power to this Gospel is prayer, and the spread of this Gospel will depend on prayer. The energy which was to give it marvelous momentum and conquering power over all its malignant and powerful foes is the energy of prayer.

The fortunes of the kingdom of Jesus Christ are not made by the feebleness of its foes. They are strong and bitter and have ever been strong, and ever will be. But mighty prayer—this is the one great spiritual force which will enable the Lord Jesus Christ to enter into full possession of His kingdom, and secure for Him the heathen as His inheritance, and the uttermost part of the earth for His possession.

It is prayer which will enable Him to break His foes with a rod of iron, that will make these foes tremble in their pride and power, who are but frail potter's vessels, to be broken in pieces by one stroke of His hand. A person who can pray is the mightiest instrument Christ has in this world. A praying Church is stronger than all the gates of hell.

God's decree for the glory of His Son's kingdom is dependent on prayer for its fulfilment: "Ask of me, and I will give thee the heathen for thy inheritance, and the uttermost part of the earth for thy possession." God the Father gives nothing to His Son only through prayer. And the reason why the Church has not received more in the missionary

work in which it is engaged is the lack of prayer.
" Ye have not, because ye ask not."

Every dispensation foreshadowing the coming of
Christ when the world has been evangelised, at the
end of time, rests upon these constitutional provisions, God's decree, His promises and prayer.
However far away that day of victory by distance
or time, or remoteness of shadowy type, prayer is
the essential condition on which the dispensation
becomes strong, typical and representative. From
Abraham, the first of the nation of the Israelites,
the friend of God, down to this dispensation of the
Holy Spirit, this has been true.

> " The nations call! from sea to sea
>    Extends the thrilling cry,
> ' Come over, Christians, if there be,
>    And help us, ere we die.'
>
> " Our hearts, O Lord, the summons feel;
>    Let hand with heart combine ,
> And answer to the world's appeal,
>    By giving ' that is thine.' "

Our Lord's plan for securing workers in the
foreign missionary field is the same plan He set
on foot for obtaining preachers. It is by the
process of praying. It is the prayer plan as dis-
tinguished from all man-made plans. These mission workers are to be " sent men." God must
send them. They are God-called, divinely moved
to this great work. They are inwardly moved to

enter the harvest fields of the world and gather sheaves for the heavenly garners. Men do not choose to be missionaries any more than they choose to be preachers. God sends out labourers in His harvest fields in answer to the prayers of His Church. Here is the Divine plan as set forth by our Lord:

" But when he saw the multitudes, he was moved with compassion on them, because they fainted, and were as sheep having no shepherd. Then saith he unto his disciples, The harvest truly is plenteous, but the labourers are few. Pray ye, therefore, the Lord of the harvest that he will send forth labourers into his harvest."

It is the business of the home church to do the praying. It is the Lord's business to call and send forth the labourers. The Lord does not do the praying. The Church does not do the calling. And just as our Lord's compassions were aroused by the sight of multitudes, weary, hungry, and scattered, exposed to evils, as sheep having no shepherd, so whenever the Church has eyes to see the vast multitudes of earth's inhabitants, descendants of Adam, weary in soul, living in darkness, and wretched and sinful, will it be moved to compassion, and begin to pray the Lord of the harvest to send forth labourers into His harvest.

Missionaries, like ministers, are born of praying people. A praying church begets labourers in the harvest-field of the world. The scarcity of missionaries argues a non-praying church. It is all right to send trained men to the foreign field, but first of all they must be God-sent. The sending is the fruit of prayer. As praying men are the occasion of sending them, so in turn the workers must be praying men. And the prime mission of these praying missionaries is to convert prayerless heathen men into praying men. Prayer is the proof of their calling, their Divine credentials, and their work.

He who is not a praying man at home needs the one fitness to become a mission worker abroad. He who has not the spirit which moves him toward sinners at home, will hardly have a spirit of compassion for sinners abroad. Missionaries are not made of men who are failures at home. He who will be a man of prayer abroad must, before anything else, be a man of prayer in his home church. If he be not engaged in turning sinners away from their prayerless ways at home, he will hardly succeed in turning away the heathen from their prayerless ways. In other words, it takes the same spiritual qualifications for being a home worker as it does for being a foreign worker.

God in His own way, in answer to the prayers of His Church, calls men into His harvest-fields. Sad will be the day when Missionary Boards and Churches overlook that fundamental fact, and send out their own chosen men independent of God.

Is the harvest great? Are the labourers few? Then "pray ye the Lord of the harvest to send forth labourers into his harvest." Oh, that a great wave of prayer would sweep over the Church asking God to send out a great army of labourers into the needy harvest fields of the earth! No danger of the Lord of the harvest sending out too many labourers and crowding the fields. He who calls will most certainly provide the means for supporting those whom He calls and sends forth.

The one great need in the modern missionary movement is intercessors. They were scarce in the days of Isaiah. This was his complaint:

" And he saw that there was no man, and wondered that there was no intercessor."

So today there is great need of intercessors, first, for the needy harvest-fields of earth, born of a Christly compassion for the thousands without the Gospel; and then intercessors for labourers to be sent forth by God into the needy fields of earth.